BOUNCING BACK

Michael Flynn, aka Mattress Mick, is an Irish personality and household name. He is renowned for his bold and unconventional guerrilla marketing strategies, and his journey from bankruptcy to online sensation has captivated national audiences. In 2016, *Mattress Men*, a film that went on to win an IFTA Award, was released to widespread acclaim.

BOUNCING BACK

Memoirs of a Mattress Salesman

MATTRESS MICK

(AKA MICHAEL FLYNN)
WRITTEN BY JOSEPHINE McCAFFREY

Gill Books

Gill Books
Hume Avenue
Park West
Dublin 12
www.gillbooks.ie

Gill Books is an imprint of M.H. Gill and Co.

978 18045 8385 2

Design origination by Bartek Janczak
Edited by Miriam Mulcahy
Proofread by Liza Costello
Printed and bound in the UK using 100% renewable electricity at
CPI Group (UK) Ltd
© Ger O'Connor, 165; © Colm Quinn, 1, 175; © Collins Photo
Agency, 217
This book is typeset in Adobe Garamond Pro by
Palimpsest Book Production Ltd, Falkirk, Stirlingshire

*The paper used in this book comes from the wood pulp of
sustainably managed forests.*

*To the best of our knowledge, this book complies in full with the
requirements of the General Product Safety Regulation (GPSR).
For further information and help with any safety queries,
please contact us at productsafety@gill.ie.*

A CIP catalogue record for this book is available from
the British Library.

5 4 3 2 1

MIX
Paper | Supporting
responsible forestry
FSC www.fsc.org FSC® C013604

This book is dedicated to the memory of
my loving wife, Margaret Flynn

Contents

Prologue

I lost almost everything in the financial crash. I had to close my chain of furniture shops; suppliers were knocking at my door; I couldn't pay the staff; debts were piling up. My pride had taken a huge knock and my coping mechanism was to wander down to the local, The Yacht in Clontarf, order a pint and just sit. I'd pour my worry into that glass and sit in deep thought. I needed an idea. Something, anything. One day, sitting there, I saw a documentary on the telly about a car salesman who'd turned himself into a celebrity. He sold cars and he sold himself. He was loud, ridiculous and very successful. That stuck with me.

So, I started digging around. Researching American retailers who became personalities. There was this fella called Mattress Mack from Houston, Texas. He started out with very little but made himself a millionaire by creating a persona called Mattress Mack.

That's when it started to click. Mattresses – that was my niche, and pretty much the only stock I had left. I knew the product inside out and still had a few solid contacts in the supply chain. Maybe I could recreate something similar here in Ireland. In a small country, drawing attention to yourself can either backfire completely or turn out to be a stroke of genius. I held on to the idea but didn't act on it yet.

A few weeks later, same pub, same drink, different day. A voice calls across: 'How are you, Mick?' I look up. No idea who it is, but I nod back and he comes over. 'You don't remember me, do you? It's Paul Kelly, used to see you in the Pearse Street shop.' I faked a smile, said, 'Of course, Paul!' and we got chatting. Paul had started his own business called Shoot Audition and he started telling me all about it.

Everything was going online, he said. Social media was the new high street, and if you weren't on it, you were basically invisible. Everyone and their dog was advertising on Facebook and YouTube. To be honest, back then, I hadn't a clue about social media. Might as well have been reading Morse code with my eyes shut. But Paul? He knew about it all from the course he was doing. He was already shooting audition tapes for actors, editing them, getting stuck into creating video content for online.

'This is where it's all going,' he told me, eyes wide with conviction. 'You need to get online. You need to use social media.' I looked at him, nodded slowly and said, 'That couldn't have come at a better time, Paul.' Because I had already started poking around the idea of branding myself like what Mattress Mack has done in America. I told Paul I was thinking of doing something along those lines and putting my own spin on it.

I liked Paul straight away. He wasn't just full of ideas, he was full of heart. He had that spark. A man on a mission. He was a devoted father, grinding every day not just for himself, but to build a better life for his kids.

A few days later – this was back in January 2010 – he sent my sister Mary an email to tell me more about what he could offer in terms of helping me market myself. Okay, I hold my hands up: I've never sent an email in my life. Answering the phone is where my technical knowledge begins and ends.

So we arranged a meeting in The Yacht, and hatched a plan. A mad plan, but a beautiful plan. We bounced names around and eventually, like some kind of divine mattress-related miracle, we landed on *Mattress Mick*. To this day we still bicker over who came up with the name. I say it was me, I was the one obsessing over Mattress Mack after all. Paul swears blind it was him. Who knows? All I know is, that moment in the pub is when Mattress Mick was born.

And something in me clicked. I got excited. I thought, *this could actually work*. This could be the thing to change everything around. We brainstormed how I'd present myself. Should we get an actor to play me? Maybe an animated cartoon version of myself? Eventually, we decided: why look further than the real deal? I was cheaper, funnier, and if I do say so myself, better-looking.

In 2012, I registered the name Mattress Mick. I set out to become Ireland's number one mattress salesman. Whether you needed memory foam, a latex mattress, or even a sofa bed, I was going to be your man. My mission was simple: to make sure the country got a great night's sleep and, in the process, to become the Mattress King. And maybe, just maybe, if I pulled it off, I'd finally get a good night's sleep myself. And so it began.

Chapter 1

Pearse Street Boy

We have seen his star shining in the south side. He shall be born on 21 February 1951. Many came from far and wide to witness this miracle birth, mainly from Pearse Street, Dublin City Centre. He will be known and hailed throughout the land for all eternity as Michael Flynn, King of the Mattresses.

I came into the world on 21 February 1951 in Chapelizod, a quiet little suburb of Dublin, and a year later, my brother Brian was born. Not that I remember much of it as we didn't stay there long after I was born. Before I knew it, we'd moved to Landscape Park, in Churchtown, D14, which was a rising and respectable part of Dublin at the time. My sisters Mary and Catherine were born in that house. That's where I spent most of my formative years, learning about life, people and the unpredictable nature of both.

My parents, Larry and Catherine Flynn, were salt-of-the-earth people. My mother, Catherine, was a real character, larger than life, and loved by everyone. She had a laugh that could wake the dead and a heart that would give to anyone in need.

They met in the most timeless way, like so many good Catholics of their generation did, in church. At the Immaculate Heart of Mary Church on City Quay in Dublin. While most came for prayers and sermons, I've a feeling my dad's devotion was aimed more towards a certain young woman sitting a few pews in front of him than towards the altar.

In fact my father Larry had his eye on my mother Catherine for quite some time. And though he'd never admit it outright, I don't think it was religious fervour that kept him showing up so faithfully week after week. It was the hope of catching just a glimpse of her. My mother was, by all accounts, breathtaking.

Back then, in the late 1940s, my mother worked as a millinery model. She turned heads everywhere she went. It sounds as though every man who passed her on Grafton Street had his heart stop when she walked by. But my father was different. He didn't just want to admire her from afar, he wanted to ask her out. There was, however, a bit of competition.

At the time, Mam was already seeing someone, the owner of Fitzpatrick's shoe shop on Grafton Street, a dapper sort of fellow who had taken a shine to her during one of her modelling jobs. They courted for a while, and I imagine they made quite the elegant pair. But that didn't faze my father.

He was patient, persistent and quietly romantic. Week after week, he'd turn up at Mass, dressed immaculately, suit pressed, hair slicked, shoes polished, sitting just close enough to be noticed, but never so bold as to intrude. He waited, watched and hoped. Eventually, he summoned the courage to ask her out. And when he did, she turned him down.

But he wasn't a man who gave up and he came back, again and again. Sunday after Sunday, like clockwork. Not with grand declarations or flashy gestures, but with unwavering intention and the hope of even just friendship. And something in that gentle determination must have changed something in my mother.

The second time he asked, she said yes. I'm not sure what happened with the shoe salesman, but he was long forgotten by this point. That one little word changed everything. It was the beginning of Larry and Catherine, a love story rooted not in whirlwind passion, but in steadfast devotion. In glances exchanged beneath the high ceilings of a church, in footsteps echoing on cobbled streets, in the slow, graceful unfolding of two lives winding their way towards one another.

And once they came together, they stayed that way. Through laughter and tears, good days and bad, hand in hand. It's a love that still lingers in the air when we speak their names. Maybe the kind of love that begins in a church pew lasts a lifetime.

My mother's family owned a pub on Sir John Rogerson's Quay in the heart of Dublin, it was a lively hub of city life known as Smyths. It was the kind of place where stories were told, laughter echoed, and the pulse of Dublin could be felt in every clink of a glass. Growing up in that environment, even if only as an observer from the stairwell, kept at a distance by her protective parents, Hannah and Austin Smyth, left a profound and lasting imprint on my mother. I believe those early experiences helped shape her warm, outgoing nature. It was in her blood, the effortless ability to connect with others, to infuse a room with energy, and to make everyone around her feel seen, valued and truly welcome.

My grandmother Hannah was song and soul. She was pure joy in human form. You couldn't say a sentence without her turning it into a song. She'd be humming, laughing, clapping her hands, her spirit was infectious. She was the kind of woman who found happiness in the simple things and made sure everyone around her felt it too. There was a softness in her, a playfulness that reminded me so much of my mother. You couldn't help but smile in her presence.

My mother always carried herself with an air of dignity and grace that never wavered, but never thought she was better than anyone else. As a millinery model, she knew how to showcase herself, wearing the finest hats with poise and sophistication. Her appearance was always impeccable, her makeup flawlessly applied, her nails perfectly manicured, and her wardrobe nothing short of stylish and refined.

Everything about her was a world apart from the Flynns' stiff upper lip. She was vibrant, warm and full of life. She had a way of making the ordinary feel extraordinary. She was the one who brought light and laughter into our home. Always putting on funny voices, doing impressions, breaking into silly characters, she turned everyday moments into little performances. It was part of her charm. Both she and my father shared a deep love for the theatre. They adored it, drama, performance, storytelling, it was a thread that tied them together. They often went to plays, and when they couldn't, they brought the show home. I remember them dancing in the kitchen, swirling around the tiled floor to old records, laughing like they were the only two people in the world. And they taught us to dance too, spinning us around the room like we were part of some whimsical family musical. There was no shortage of theatrics in our household. Among life's hardship and loss there was some joy, and I suppose that explains a lot about me.

Regardless of our financial circumstances, she never allowed her presentation to falter. Whether dressed in the latest fashions or making do with what she had, she exuded confidence and charm, a testament to her unwavering sense of self-respect that I inherited from her and carry with me throughout the ups and downs of my life.

As parents went at the time, she was easy-going enough, never one to rule with an iron fist, and maybe that's exactly why my siblings, Brian, Mary and Catherine, or I never felt the need to rebel. There was no oppressive authority to push back against, just a steady hand guiding us along. That's not to say we didn't have our moments, every child back then knew the sting of a slipper at least once but discipline was never harsh.

We were all raised Catholic and went to church like most families, but unlike some, we weren't brought up with the fear of God looming over us. Religion was part of our lives, but it wasn't a heavyweight. We believed, but we weren't afraid. In 1958, I made my First Holy Communion, a monumental day in any young boy's life, especially back then. I was bursting with excitement, practically hyperventilating with anticipation because, for once, the spotlight was mine. I knew I'd be spoiled, and even at that age, I was never one to shy away from a bit of attention. But just as I was gearing up for my big moment, something even more exciting happened, something that completely stole my thunder. My sister, Catherine, was born. Suddenly, my special day was overshadowed, and I was not happy about it. My Communion was instantly bumped to second place, and to this day, I'm not sure I've entirely forgiven her.

My father, Larry Flynn, was quite a character, a small, slim man with a distinctive presence. Struggling with severe asthma from a young age, he missed out on many of the experiences a young fella should have and that defined his youth. His parents, Ellen and Michael, were tough on him, they were cut from a different cloth than my own. My grandparents suffered the heartbreaking loss of a son when he was only the tender age of 10 years old and I believe that tragedy changed them. That kind of grief hardens people, and in their case, it made them even stricter. My grandfather Michael was a strong, formidable man, the kind who could sell sand in the desert. In contrast, my father was gentler, deeply honest, and a man of quiet integrity. But in my grandfather's eyes, that gentleness was a weakness, a softness that created an unspoken, unhealed divide between them, shaping an unspoken but undeniable distance in their relationship.

Looking back, I realise how much I've inherited from all of them. From my grandmother Ellen, the fierce pride and resilience. From my father, the belief in dignity through struggle. From my mother, a love of joy, drama and finding beauty in the everyday. And from Granny Hannah, the music, the laughter, that has always played in the background of my life.

Dad was the heart and soul of our family. I believe he loved us with such pride and devotion because he wanted to ensure we never felt the way his own parents had made him feel. Some of my fondest memories are of him taking us to South William Street to pick up stock for my grandparents' shop. He would always stop at a little cake shop, beaming with pride as he showed us all off. He truly idolised us, and he was such a joy to be around. I can still picture my sisters playing dress-up, twirling around the kitchen as he danced with them, laughing and carefree. He was determined to be a different kind of father, one full of warmth, fun and love, a far cry from the one he had known.

My father was also deeply woven into the fabric of the community. He worked in my grandad's shop, Mickey Flynn's, on Pearse Street. In 1936, my grandparents, Michael and Ellen Flynn, leased the shop at 73 Pearse Street and transformed it into a bustling hub that sold just about everything. More than just a store, it became a gathering place, a lifeline for the community, and a testament to our family's hardworking spirit. In its early days, the shop specialised in fishing gear, waders and yellow jackets, making it the first stop for fishermen returning from sea. After stepping off their trawlers, they would head straight to Mickey Flynn's before being directed to my mother's family pub, Smyths.

Churchtown and Pearse Street felt like worlds apart back then. Churchtown was a safe, friendly place where we could run freely as children, while Pearse Street was a completely different story. Dad would come home from the shop on Pearse Street exhausted, but we always looked forward to his return. He never failed to bring back wild stories about the people he met and the things he had witnessed that day.

As a child in Churchtown, my days were filled with the pure joy of freedom, playing football on the streets with my two best pals, Frankie O'Rourke and Austin Colley. Though Austin has since passed, the bond we shared remained strong throughout the years. Our local was Young's, the sweet shop; Smarties and pastilles were my tipple at the time. We were good kids for the most part, never causing too much trouble except for the occasional mischief of sneaking into a neighbour's garden to steal apples and conkers. That was about as rebellious as we ever got at that stage. Yes, in my parents' eyes, I was an absolute angel.

At just 10 years old, I got my first taste of the working world. I used to watch the milkman make his deliveries, hopping on and off his slow-moving, battery-operated float. One day, I decided to jump on and help, grabbing the milk and placing it at people's doors, saving him time and effort. Determined to make it official, I marched down to HB Dairies in Rathfarnham and landed my first job as a milk boy, helping with the morning rounds. Even then, I loved the idea of being up early and out working. I did three mornings a week, and I earned about two shillings. I was the big man and the sweets were on me. I was the only one among my friends with a job, and I'll never forget the pride of earning my own money, even if most of it ended up across the counter at Young's sweet shop.

When we lived in Churchtown, my primary school was St Louis in Rathmines, which was run by the nuns. We were lucky because you'd often hear horror stories about strict nuns and Christian Brothers in other schools, but we never experienced anything like that. In fact, I have fond memories of the nuns, which isn't the usual story people would tell. One in particular, Sister Gemma, was my favourite. She had a warm, friendly smile, a far cry from the strict and stern nuns who filled the halls of other schools. At the end of every class, Sister Gemma would hand out sweets, bringing a little joy to the end of each day. I think I was a little in love with Sister Gemma, I think we all were. Overall, my years in Churchtown left me with wonderful childhood memories, but all of that was about to change.

In 1962, when I was 11, the shop on Pearse Street ran into serious trouble. My grandparents, Ellen and Michael, were on the brink of losing everything they had worked for. My grandfather had amassed a huge debt, much of it, I believe, driven by extravagance, and a desire to impress. The Flynn family carried themselves with a kind of pride that often teetered into snobbery. But behind the velvet curtains of their refined self-image lay a mountain of debt and dysfunction. They lived beyond their means, convinced their name and status could mask reality. My grandfather, Mickey Flynn, was no pillar of virtue. No one ever said it outright, but it was well understood that he was something of a womaniser.

He was the type of man who always wore pristine white suits, always out on the town, always chasing something, skirts, dreams, maybe both. He had this air of glamour and grandeur, but underneath it all, he was reckless. His spending habits and lifestyle were largely to blame for the family's financial mess. And yet, despite all that, they carried themselves as if they were royalty.

He loved the finer things in life, spending lavishly on expensive cars and grand weddings for my aunts. One married a doctor, the other an engineer and, for Mickey, that was a source of immense pride.

When my father brought my mother home for the first time, she looked every bit the part, elegant, poised and undeniably beautiful. On the surface, she fit seamlessly into the world they had built. But beneath the polished appearance, she was still the daughter of a publican, and to my father's family, that lineage simply didn't align with the image they so carefully cultivated. They saw it as beneath them, socially inferior and unworthy of the prestige they believed they held.

They were businesspeople, proud and status-conscious, eager to brag about how successfully their children had married. It was part of the brand, part of the legacy they wanted to leave behind. So, when their golden boy, Larry, fell in love with and chose to marry a publican's daughter, it was met not with joy, but with thinly veiled disappointment. In their eyes, it was a scandal. Almost laughable now, really, how something as simple as love could be considered such a threat to the family's social standing.

That one decision to marry my mother cast a long shadow. It was seen as a misstep that didn't fit the narrative they were so desperate to tell the world. And yet, the irony is hard to ignore: my mother's family was far more financially stable than the Flynns ever were. While the Flynns chased status and accumulated debt, her family ran a successful business and lived within their means.

My grandfather wanted to show the world that we were just as good as anyone else, but that kind of status came at a steep price. Keeping up with the Joneses wasn't just expensive, it nearly cost him everything. The shop wasn't just a business – it was like an extension of our family and losing it would have been a heartbreaking blow.

In a desperate bid to stay afloat, my grandfather persuaded my father to sell our family home in Churchtown to help settle some of his debts. It was an agonising decision, especially for my parents, who adored that house, none more so than my mother. It was clear my father didn't give in willingly, but whatever was said behind closed doors left him with no real choice. In the end, he sacrificed the home they had built together, a decision that weighed heavily on him. But for my mother, it was devastating. She was forced to leave behind the order and comfort of her own home, where everything was just as she liked it, and forced to step into complete chaos, a shattering change.

It was 1962 when we left Churchtown, and it's a night I will never forget. It was late, far later than you'd expect for a move. Maybe my parents wanted to leave quietly, without too much attention from the neighbours. I remember our Morris Minor packed to the brim, every inch filled, while the four of us squeezed into the backseat. The air was heavy with something unspoken.

That moment marked a turning point. We left behind the peace and beauty of our idyllic suburban life and were thrust into the chaos of Pearse Street, right in the heart of the city.

Seventy-three Pearse Street was nothing like the life I had known, it was more *Steptoe and Son* than *Frawleys and Co.* As children, we rarely visited the shop – my parents felt the area was a bit rough at the time. Now it was going to be our home. The shop itself was long and narrow, with counters running along both sides. One side catered to men, stocked with workwear, trawler gear, wellies, hats, ties, socks and sturdy coats. The other side was dedicated to women, filled with aprons, tights, dresses, cardigans, ribbons and an endless array of haberdashery. Then through to the stock room and up the stairs into our new home.

I remember the house feeling dark and heavy, with large, imposing doors that made it seem even smaller. The reality of what lay ahead quickly sank in, nine people crammed into a two-bedroom home. For a young boy, it was nothing short of a nightmare.

Brian, Mary and Catherine shared a bed in my parents' room, while I was placed with my grandfather Mickey and Uncle Larry, an 'honorary' uncle. To this day, I'm still not entirely sure what his story was. The situation was even more confusing with two Larrys and two Michaels all living under one roof. Meanwhile, my grandmother Ellen took over the sitting room, claiming it as her own space. Chaos became our new normal, a situation no one was happy with.

The moment you stepped out onto the street, the thick scent of gas from the gasometer on the docks hit you like a punch. It seeped into your senses, almost knocking you off your feet. Though this was one of the poorer parts of Dublin, you never saw homelessness like you do today. Instead, the area was packed with overcrowded tenements, sometimes 14 or 15 people crammed into a single flat. That's why the streets were always alive with children. The home wasn't much more than a place to sleep and refuel before heading back out onto the street again.

Back then, your address was everything. It wasn't just where you lived; it was your identity. It told the world who you were, and Pearse Street was not the kind of place you'd want to be known for at the time.

I will never forget my first night on Pearse Street. I was crammed into a tiny, freezing room, a stark contrast to the cosy warmth of my bedroom back in Churchtown. In the dead of night, I jolted upright, my heart pounding. The walls were so thin it felt like I was in the room next door, where a couple was locked in a vicious argument. There was a loud clatter, like pots and pans being flung across the room. A woman's voice rang out, harsh and angry: 'I'll bleedin' kill ya! Get the fuck out of my sight!'

A deep male voice roared back, 'You're nothing but an auld bitch, fuck off!'

The shouting continued, insult after insult, echoing through the walls. This was life now, being forced to listen to an inner-city Dublin tragedy unfold when I should have been sleeping. That was the moment I knew that I wasn't in Kansas any more.

Part of me resented my grandparents and parents for letting this happen and for turning our worlds upside down and another part of me admired them, especially my dad. Seeing the lengths he would go to in order to survive and the sacrifices he was willing to make for his family filled me with respect. I was at an impressionable age when everything changed; my biggest concern was my image and how I fitted in with my peers, and this upheaval turned my world upside down. I think this move upset my brother Brian and sister Mary more because they were old enough to recognise the change but not fully understand why it happened. Catherine, on the other hand, was too young to notice any difference.

My siblings and I always got along well but moving in with my grandparents shifted the entire dynamic of our family life. My grandmother, Ellen Flynn, was a force to be reckoned with; she was stern, perpetually grumpy, and stuck in her old-fashioned ways, a stark contrast to my mother's more modern outlook. Every time I walked into a room, I could feel the weight of her disapproval, a silent hostility that needed no explanation.

Ellen tried to instil in us from a very young age that no matter what your circumstances were, no matter how little you had in your pocket, you held your head high. You maintained appearances. Dignity wasn't about money, it was about poise, about never letting the cracks show. She believed, fiercely, that appearances were everything.

Even if you couldn't afford dinner, you didn't let the neighbours know. You didn't speak of your struggles. You dressed well, you walked tall, and you smiled. It was a facade, yes, but it was one she wore like armour. In many ways, she was the embodiment of the old saying, 'fur coat and no knickers'. Elegance on the outside, grit and hustle underneath. She tried to make us believe that we were better than everyone else, regardless of what went on behind closed doors. Extreme confidence, sometimes bordering on delusion, was what she tried to impart.

That mentality, I think, seeped into my father too. He absorbed that sense of pride and privacy. 'Never let them see you struggle' could've been his personal motto. It was all about composure, pride and image.

My dad knew Pearse Street like the back of his hand, but that didn't stop him from worrying about us. He was a born worrier; I am too. That trait has definitely been passed down. He fretted about us being out on the street, knowing we were innocent about the rougher edges of the world, especially in that part of town. Being the new kids on the block meant we attracted curiosity, which unsettled him. He couldn't relax until we were all home safe. And he wasn't wrong. Every time we stepped outside, we felt the stares. I wasn't just another face, I was Mickey Flynn's grandson. In a place where so many struggled to get by, my life must have seemed gilded by comparison. In their eyes, I was the boy with the silver shoes.

Over time, we muddled along as best we could. Mam was a hard worker and quickly immersed herself in the shop, taking charge of the women's section. Keeping busy seemed to be a welcome distraction and escape for her. She genuinely enjoyed getting to know the locals and making new friends, and the customers adored her.

Her accent, however, would shift noticeably and go up a few octaves whenever the actresses from the Gaiety Theatre came in. She absolutely loved those visits. I think, deep down, she secretly would have loved to tread the boards herself. Maureen Potter and Rosaleen Linehan were regular customers, and Mam felt honoured to serve them. During these encounters, every 'T' and 'H' was carefully pronounced, quite a contrast to the more relaxed version of herself that she was with the locals.

To escape the close quarters of no. 73, my mother and I liked to feed the birds by the Daniel O'Connell statue on O'Connell Street. We'd go down in the morning with bits of bread. That was something we loved doing together. It was one of those lovely, quiet moments we shared as mother and son. No big trips, no money needed, just a bit of bread and time together meant everything and it also meant she could escape for a bit. I still feed the birds to this day; whenever I have a bit of dinner left over from the night before, I take it down to the shop, and the seagulls swarm. It's a simple thing that takes me back to those mornings with my mother and gives me great joy.

After spending a few years in Pearse Street, things eventually changed. Grandad and Uncle Larry passed away. They had lived long, full lives, and in many ways, their time had come. But even though their passing wasn't unexpected, it sent a ripple through the house. The dynamic shifted, and so did the space we lived in.

Suddenly, mine and Brian's room was transformed, a real boys' room, just for the two of us. It was no longer just a place to sleep; it became our own little world where we could play, dream and be ourselves. My two sisters still shared a room with Mam and Dad, while Ellen continued to dominate the living room.

At that age, we were too young to grasp the depth of loss. All we saw was the newfound space, the freedom to just be kids. I remember Brian and I setting up the biggest Scalextric track we could imagine, stretching it all the way from our room into my parents' bedroom. It was chaos, but it was magic. We were in our element, lost in the thrill of it. There was no way we could have done anything like that when Grandad and Uncle Larry were still around. Their presence had been strong, unmovable, an unspoken set of rules that dictated how we lived, how we moved. Without them, the house felt different. Lighter, somehow.

My grandmother, on the other hand, was still very much a force in the house. She made frequent trips to Roscommon to visit her sister, and we all lived for those days when she'd leave. The second she stepped out the door, sometimes before she even fully left the shop, my siblings and I would spring into action. It was like a perfectly rehearsed routine. We'd rush into the living room, fold up her bed, and transform the space back into what it was meant to be, a proper sitting room, free from her looming presence.

The truth was, she was a burden. It sounds harsh, but she was just never very pleasant to be around. Her energy hung over the house like a dark cloud, heavy and oppressive. And as soon as she was gone, it was as if the whole place could breathe again. There was a complete shift in the atmosphere, like a weight had been lifted, and we could finally relax. We never said it out loud, but we all felt it.

By the time I was 14, I was always thinking, always scheming, always looking for something to do. My mind never rested. I liked having a plan, something to work towards, and I suppose, in a way, my siblings looked up to me for that. If I'm being honest, I was a little pampered.

Whenever I was heading out, my sister Mary would make sure I looked the part. She'd iron my shirt, fix my collar, and most importantly, do my hair. I've always been fixated on my hair, obsessed with getting it just right. Even now, I still am. But back then, there was only one person I trusted to touch it and that was Mary. She just knew how I liked it, the exact way to style it. My hair was and still is very distinctive, almost like my calling card. Big, bouncy waves that blow in the breeze. You don't see me coming; you see my hair arriving five seconds before I do.

Looking back, those were the days, the mid-sixties, that shaped us. We didn't have much, but we had each other. The house behind the shop was small, sometimes chaotic and often stifling. But it was ours. And even in the moments of tension, in the lingering presence of grief, in the shadow of old rules and expectations, we still found ways to be kids. To carve out space for joy. To make our own little world within it all even under the disapproving gaze of Granny Ellen.

Chapter 2

Synge Street Brothers

Synge Street was my secondary school, and I got on well with all my classmates. Despite being in Dublin 8, it pulled pupils in from places like Rathmines, Donnybrook or Sandymount, places that were seen as better. I was different, the outsider. I was the Pearse Street boy.

There were eight of us in our group, Mal Deveney, Joe Byrne, Shane Flynn, Paddy Pounch, Freddie Reynolds, Barry Murray and Sean Cusack, with Mal and Joe as my closest mates. Sadly, Shane and Paddy have since passed, but to this day, the rest of us are all still good friends. I have never had a falling out with any of them, and we meet for a Christmas lunch every year.

Back then, dances were held in tennis clubs and were the place to be at the time, with Lansdowne being the main one. Everyone went. You needed a membership card to get in, and that card had your address on it. That alone decided who was welcome and who wasn't. The moment they saw 'Pearse Street,' the answer was always the same: no.

It stung. No matter how much I tried to fit in, no matter how close I was with my friends, there were places I simply wasn't allowed to go. But what meant the most, what softened the blow, was my friends. Every time I was turned away, they didn't just leave me standing there alone. They refused to go in without me. One by one, they'd walk away in an almost silent protest, choosing loyalty over a night of dancing. That gesture, simple but profound, stayed with me. It meant everything to know that, even in a world that tried to keep me on the outside, I had great friends who wouldn't let me be left behind.

My friends and I weren't troublemakers by any means, but we were a tight-knit group with a bond that ran deep. We didn't cause chaos or stir up trouble; instead, we focused on enjoying life in our own way. We spent our days together, always out on some adventure, finding fun in the simplest things. Whether we were wandering the streets, hanging out at the park, or just messing around, we always had each other's backs. If one of us found ourselves in a tough spot, the others were right there, no questions asked, ready to step in. It wasn't about being rebellious or pushing boundaries; it was about loyalty, friendship and the unspoken understanding that no matter what, we had each other's support through thick and thin.

Synge Street was run by the Christian Brothers. Now, Christian Brothers didn't quite mean priests, it meant something worse. They had authority, but not the sanctity that came with priesthood, and I think that gave them a deep-seated inferiority complex. A frustration they took out on us. Their weapon of choice? A thick leather strap, designed specifically for beating young boys into submission.

We were used to it. The sting of leather across our hands, arms, even our backs, it was routine. We never told our parents. It wasn't worth it. This was just how things were. If you spoke out of turn, copied your mate's work, or so much as breathed the wrong way, you'd get the strap. It was normal.

Until one day, it wasn't.

That day is burned into my memory.

We were sitting in class, restless as always, but behaving. The Christian Brother had stepped out for a moment, leaving us unsupervised. Our school backed onto the main road, and suddenly, out of nowhere, a woman walked in. Not just any woman but a beautiful woman. She was lost, looking for directions, and we, a pack of hormone-fuelled teenage boys in an all-boys school, lost our minds.

It was chaos. Jeering, cheering, shouting, banging on desks, you'd think we'd never seen a real woman before. But then, the door swung open. One of the Christian Brothers walked in. I can't remember his name, but I will *never* forget his face. His expression twisted into something primal. He didn't just look angry, he looked like a man possessed. The young woman barely had time to realise what was happening before he yanked her out of the room, showing her the way she was supposed to go. Then he came back, his face red, his breath ragged.

And then he snapped.

His scream cut through the room like a knife. It wasn't just shouting, it was pure, unfiltered rage, something beyond discipline or authority. It was the kind of anger that seeps into your bones, that makes the air too thick to breathe. Then he locked eyes on one of my classmates, Billy. The poor lad never got a chance to react before the Brother was on him. He grabbed him and threw him across the room like a ragdoll. Billy hit the ground hard, but there was no time to recover. The Brother was on top of him, beating him relentlessly. Fist, strap, whatever he could use, he just kept hitting and hitting so furiously, he looked possessed.

The room was silent. No one dared move, let alone speak. If we did, we knew we'd be next. We watched in horror as

Billy's body went limp. Then, someone broke. One of the boys sprinted out of the room, ran down the hall and called for an ambulance.

Billy was barely conscious by the time the paramedics arrived. He was beaten that badly. Nearly at death's door, they said. And yet, somehow, the school managed to twist it, to justify it. Billy had deserved it. This was discipline. Billy never came back. Whatever he did to him that day, Billy's time at Synge Street was over. But the Brother? That fucker was back in class the very next day as if nothing had happened.

After that, the strap felt almost like merciful punishment – so mild that we nearly welcomed it after witnessing what real brutality they were capable of. It was just another part of school life, something to be endured and, in a strange way, even embraced.

My friends and I would often compare the red marks on our hands, turning it into a sort of competition to see who had taken the worst hit, whose mark lasted the longest, and who didn't flinch. It became almost a badge of honour, a shared experience that bonded us rather than broke us. Looking back now, it's odd to think how casually we accepted it, how we shrugged off something that today would be unthinkable. But back then, we didn't question it. That was just how things were, and we carried on, laughing and talking, always talking, no matter how many times we got the strap for it.

Paddy was the one who seemed to get the most straps for talking. If anyone had a knack for pushing the limits, it was him. He was definitely the cheekiest among us, outspoken to the point where he couldn't always help himself. But oddly enough, Paddy was also the one who hated getting the strap the most.

One particular day during class, Brother Crotty, who wasn't one of the worst ones, was teaching. We were all sitting quietly, at least, we were supposed to be, but that changed when Paddy started laughing. It wasn't just any laugh. Once Paddy started, he couldn't stop for love nor money. He was one of those who just couldn't hold it in. And that day, something set him off. Brother Crotty was teaching about original sin, and how sexual intercourse should only take place within holy matrimony. Hearing a Brother talk about sexual intercourse got the better of Paddy. Maybe it was the awkwardness of the subject or the way Brother Crotty phrased it, but once the giggles started, there was no stopping him.

All we could hear was a muffled, desperate laugh that Paddy was struggling, unsuccessfully, to suppress. His shoulders trembled, and his face turned bright red as he fought with everything he had to keep from bursting into laughter in the middle of the lesson. In a last-ditch attempt to hide himself, he ducked under his desk, but even that couldn't stop the inevitable. The laugh kept bubbling up and became uncontrollably loud. The rest of us, of course, could hardly hold back our own laughter as we watched him fight it. We all knew it was only a matter of time before Brother Crotty noticed. And sure enough, he did.

Brother Crotty's eyes locked onto Paddy, and he was called up to the front of the class.

'Do you find this subject funny?' Brother Crotty roared.

Poor Paddy, head bowed in shame and still trying to hold back his giggles, weakly replied, 'No, Brother.' His eyes desperately avoided ours because we all knew that if he looked at us, it would be game over.

Brother Crotty instructed him to put his hand out, and Paddy, nervous as anything, did so, his hand shaking. We could see the fear written all over his face, but what really had us on edge was whether he would flinch, cry or pull his hand away. To us, it was almost like a sport, and Paddy, without fail, was always the worst at it.

It was almost as if Brother Crotty knew exactly what was going on, what we were all waiting for. Like he had become a game show host, drawing out the suspense for all it was worth. As the strap came down, something seemed to snap in Paddy. Out of nowhere, he straightened up, suddenly standing with a steel-like resolve. He knew exactly what we were all expecting, and he was determined not to give it to us.

Paddy stood with his hand held out. He didn't cry, didn't flinch, didn't pull it away. He stood there with a quiet but fierce determination, as though some invisible force had taken him over. His face showed no sign of surrender, and we were all left in awe. When it was over, he slowly raised his hand to show the class the red marks, almost as if he were proudly declaring his own victory. The room erupted into cheers, a wave of admiration flooding the class. For that brief moment, Paddy was a hero, well, at least for the day. Even Crotty seemed quietly impressed, nodding in silent acknowledgement of Paddy's unexpected bravery. Paddy strutted down the classroom like he had just won a major boxing tournament.

Out of all my friends from that time, the one who truly broke my heart was Paddy. Paddy's life was already complicated before he ever joined our school. At the age of 13, he had been sent away to train as a Christian Brother. But it didn't work out, and when he came back, he was different, like something had been broken inside him. He was eager to fit in, desperate to impress us, and of course, we let him into our little gang. But there was always something off about him. Something sad.

At lunchtime, while the rest of us were messing around, Paddy would head to the chemist and buy packets of Pro Plus caffeine tablets. He was always searching for something, something to numb himself, something to take the edge off. He was highly strung, jittery, like he was constantly trying to outrun something we couldn't see. We didn't ask questions. We didn't understand, not then.

Pro Plus turned to pot. And pot? Well, nobody thought much of it back then. Everyone smoked a bit. But Paddy didn't just smoke it, he needed it. One day I was in Switzer's toilets on Grafton Street when Phil Lynott walked in. He wasn't famous yet, still only a teenager and just another lad knocking about. He came up to me and said, 'I hear your mate Paddy knows where to get pot.'

So I told him, 'Yeah, yeah, no problem, I'll ask him for you.' I went to Paddy, asked if he had anything to sell. He didn't, but he wanted the money. So, he wrapped an Oxo cube in tinfoil and sold it off as hash. I didn't even ask why he had a box of Oxo cubes in his bag, maybe for an emergency stew I jokingly thought, but it was clear he had done this before. I don't know how much he got for it, but I do know that Phil never came back looking for more.

I still have images of Phil Lynott sprinkling an Oxo cube over tobacco, and it gives me a little giggle.

Paddy was always chasing the next escape. Pot wasn't enough after a while. He moved on to the harder stuff. Heroin. He never took it around us, we never actually saw him do it, but we knew. We didn't understand drugs back then. Not really. We thought it was all just a phase, something people dabbled in. We had no idea how deep it could pull someone under. And Paddy? Paddy wasn't just chasing a high. He was trying to bury something. Something dark.

Years later, I found out the truth. The Christian Brothers had abused him when he was away. Suddenly, everything made sense. The nervous energy. The need to escape. The way he was always running from something invisible. What they did to him destroyed him. It warped his mind, his self-worth, his entire understanding of himself. He was desperate for money, always, drugs were his survival. He'd do anything for it. When I say anything, I mean anything. I think the abuse had twisted his perception of sex, of his own body, of what it all meant. Paddy wasn't gay, but he let men use him. He became, for lack of a better word, a male prostitute. I asked him once, 'Paddy, how do you do it?' He looked at me, and with a sad, hollow smile and said, 'I just close my eyes and think of Marilyn Monroe.'

Eventually, he left for London. Back then, if you were a registered heroin addict, a doctor could prescribe you free heroin. There was a Boots pharmacy near Piccadilly Circus where Paddy got his fix. He always took as little as he could of what he was prescribed so he could sell the rest to survive. But his time in London was short, and Paddy died young, way too young.

Drugs took him in the end, but really, it was the Christian Brothers who killed him. They stole his childhood, his dignity, his life. He never stood a chance. And when I think about him now, about the boy who just wanted to fit in, about the man who couldn't escape his pain, my heart shatters. By now,

I had fully realised that the Christian Brothers were, without a doubt, absolute lunatics. Mad men. I never took them seriously.

I ended up in an afterschool music group with my mates, who were all more into it than me. I just went along for the laugh. Mad Bastard Gilroy, another one of the lunatics who ran the asylum, was often there, keeping an eye on things. At one point, he walked up to me and asked me to name a musical instrument. So, without thinking, I said, 'Drums.'

He narrowed his eyes. 'Oh, so you can play the drums, can you, Michael?'

Now, obviously, I couldn't play the drums. I didn't have a musical bone in my body. But being the eejit I was, I just nodded and said, 'Yeah.' That's when he pulled out three tin cans, plonked them in front of me, handed me two rulers, and said, 'Go on then, play me a tune.' I had no idea what I was doing. I just started whacking away at these tin cans, completely clueless. It sounded like a bin rolling down a hill and my mates were in hysterics looking at me banging away on tin cans with two rulers. He watched for a few seconds, then sneered, 'I don't recognise that tune at all Michael. You're lying, you can't play the drums, can you?' And just like that, he had his excuse.

Out came the strap. A hard whack across my hand, all because I couldn't create music from the tin cans. He was a right miserable bastard. They all were. Completely unhinged and at that point I also realised I had no future as a drummer.

We were stepping well into our teenage years, growing more outspoken, more independent. I was beginning to carve out my own identity, no longer just a boy but someone finding his place in the world. With each passing day, I felt myself evolving, becoming more confident, more sure of who I was, and slowly stepping into being a man.

In those days, we spent our lunchtimes at The Bunner, just off Synge Street, a legendary spot back then and a great place to hang out. The Bunner was tucked away down a little lane, it was our go-to place to smoke, chat about football, and talk about girls. By fifth and sixth year, we were starting to come into our own, gaining a bit more confidence.

After school, we'd head into town, usually to Switzer's, which is now Brown Thomas. They had a café downstairs, a perfect meeting spot. That's where we'd run into girls from Loreto College, Stephen's Green, and other schools. It was the place to be. And it was there, in that café, that I met the first girl I ever fell in love with.

Looking back, I'm pretty sure I was the coolest kid in school, or at least that's what I told myself. Everyone wanted to be my friend. Maybe it was because I came from the wrong side of town, which automatically gave me a bit of an edge. But, of course, I played it cool, acting like I didn't notice. I was the ringleader. The fearless leader. The one who made terrible decisions first so everyone else could follow.

For example, I was the one who introduced my friends to the joys (and horrors) of drinking. I remember being 15 when I dragged my mate Joe Byrne to this absolute dive of a pub called The Schooner. The place was down by the docks, which, back then, was basically where common sense went to die. It was scruffy, sketchy and definitely not somewhere you'd take your mother. But to us? It was perfect.

We strolled in, still in our school uniforms, like we owned the place. I confidently marched up to the bar and ordered a pint of Smithwick's. Joe, clearly panicking under the pressure, spotted a picture of Harp beer behind the bar and blurted out, 'Uh … a pint of Harp, please?' The bartender, completely unfazed by the two teenage idiots before him, poured our drinks without so much as a raised eyebrow. And just like that, we had a local.

Over time, The Schooner became *the* spot. We weren't the only ones, there were always other underage kids there, also in their school uniforms, drinking away like it was the most normal thing in the world. Different times, I guess. Now, if you think *that* was the pinnacle of my bad decisions, allow me to introduce you to the time I nearly died of whiskey-fuelled stupidity.

One summer, Joe and I somehow ended up on an outing with the Legion of Mary, a religious group. Were we particularly religious? Not even slightly. But we had heard that some girls were going, so obviously we signed up immediately. The destination? Portrane Beach. Their plan? Have a holy and wholesome day out. My plan? Smuggle in a full bottle of whiskey and impress everyone with my elite drinking skills.

Once we got to the beach, I pulled out the bottle, poured myself a full glass, and offered one to Joe. He wisely declined. I, on the other hand, decided to demonstrate my toughness by necking it in one go. Joe stared at me in horror. Feeling confident, I poured another, straight down. No hesitation. No fear. No brain cells either, apparently. After the third massive glass, I glanced at the bottle and realised it was nearly gone. I felt invincible. The king of alcohol. The *Don* of whiskey. Then … I stood up.

The second the fresh sea air hit my face, my entire body shut down like an old computer. My legs betrayed me. I collapsed dramatically onto the sand, and chaos erupted.

People rushed over. Among them? A priest from our local church, who took one look at me and realised I was in serious trouble. There was no time to get me to a hospital, so they hauled my half-dead body to the nearest facility, the Central Mental Health Facility. Yep, that's right. My grand whiskey debut ended with me being rushed to a mental hospital.

They had to pump my stomach. Apparently, it was touch and go for a while. Everyone was properly worried, but to me, it was just a lesson in how *not* to drink whiskey. My parents showed up the next day, mortified. They weren't angry as much as deeply concerned that I might have a *problem*. But really, I was just an idiot trying to show off.

I made it home in one piece, thankfully. And while the whole ordeal didn't exactly put me off drinking forever, I can say with absolute certainty, I never, *ever* tried to down an entire bottle of whiskey again.

Chapter 3

Cathy

By this time, my family had truly become part of Pearse Street, so much so that we felt like part of the very walls that held it together. But the weight of my grandfather's debts still hung over us like a storm that refused to pass. Selling the house in Churchtown had barely made a dent in the mountain of what he owed, his habit of putting everything on credit leaving us trapped in a cycle of struggle. I know my father carried that guilt heavily, always trying desperately to make it up to us. But the burden of it all, the relentless worry, chipped away at him, taking its toll on his health.

Money worries aside, there was a new sense of freedom in the house after Uncle Larry and Grandad passed. It was as if the weight of the past had lifted just enough for us to breathe a little easier. And with that freedom, Pearse Street came alive in a way it never had before. It wasn't just our home any more, it became the place to be.

The back storeroom, once a forgotten space filled with odds and ends, was transformed into our own little den of laughter and late nights. People were always coming and going, the door never really closing for long. There was an energy to the place, a hive of constant movement and celebration. We threw parties for any occasion we could think of, Christmas, New Year's, birthdays, or sometimes for no reason at all. The nights stretched on endlessly, drinks in hand, music blasting, and laughter ringing through the walls until the early hours. By 5 a.m., the streets outside were a sight to behold, a parade of bleary-eyed, swaying figures stumbling their way home, the last echoes of our revelry still hanging in the air.

Dad was especially mad about the Eurovision and every year he made sure it was a proper event. He'd gather everyone around, drinks flowing, anticipation building as we waited to see who would take the crown. When Dana won it was something else. We were over the moon and cheered so loudly it probably shook the whole street, and 'All Kinds of Everything' was a melody that rang through every heart and home. Dad, in his usual grand style, decided there was only one way to celebrate, so he treated everyone to a chipper. That night has always stayed with me.

It was 1967, and the school year was winding down. Excitement hurled around inside me, I could hardly wait to step out into the real world, earn my own money, and carve my own path. I had no doubt that success was waiting for me, that I was destined to go places. After all, I'd already had a glimpse into the working world, and I was ready. Nothing was going to distract me. Well, almost nothing.

One afternoon, after school, my friends and I gathered at our usual spot, Switzer's, where we sipped weak, lukewarm coffee, the closest thing to metropolitan sophistication that Dublin had to offer back then. We were just having a laugh when the café door swung open, the bell above it jingling. Joe, sitting beside me, nudged my arm. 'Look over there,' he muttered. Two girls had just walked in, their navy school uniforms marking them as students of Dominican College on Eccles Street. But I barely noticed the second girl because the first one nearly took my breath away. She was stunning, with long blonde hair that fell over her shoulders, and the most striking blue eyes I had ever seen. She looked like something out of a film.

Joe and I dared each other to go up and talk to them, but I hesitated. I wasn't usually shy, but this time was different. I could feel the nerves creeping in, the fear of rejection holding me back. Instead, we settled for giving them a knowing nod as they walked past, and after 20 minutes or so they were gone. I kicked myself afterwards, regretting my hesitation, and of course the lads had a great time teasing me for it. I laughed along, but deep down, I couldn't shake the feeling that I had just let someone special pass me by.

From that day on, I made sure to be in Switzer's nearly every afternoon, hoping she would come back. Two weeks passed, and still, there was no sign of her. Each day, I walked into Switzer's with a mix of hope and disappointment, scanning the café for that familiar face, but she was nowhere to be seen. I began to lose hope, telling myself that it had been a one-time chance, and I had blown it.

Then, on a quiet Tuesday afternoon, I was sitting with my mates, half-listening to their usual banter, when the café door opened and there she was. My heart nearly stopped, again. For a second, I couldn't move. I just stared, hardly believing my luck. This was it, another chance. I wasn't going to waste it. This time, I was determined. No bottling it. No letting nerves get the better of me. She walked in, glancing around before taking a seat at a table on the other side of the café. My moment had arrived. As I took a deep breath and stood up, my mates caught on to what was happening. 'Go on, Michael,' one of them whispered. Another started a slow, dramatic build-up hum, and within seconds, the whole table had joined in, egging me on like I was about to step into a boxing ring.

'Ah, shut up, will ye?' I muttered, trying to keep my composure as I walked towards her, doing my best to appear confident. I stopped at her table, my heart thudding in my chest.

'Hello,' I said. She looked up, her blue eyes bright with curiosity, and then she smiled.

'Hello,' she replied. Phew. So far, so good. In those days, things were different. You didn't just walk up to someone and start chatting like people do now. Courting was more formal, we took our time, got to know each other. But at that moment, I decided not to wait. I just went for it.

'Would you like to go to the pictures with me?' I asked, forcing my voice to stay steady despite the nerves rattling inside me. Then came what felt like the longest silence in the history of mankind. She looked at me, I braced myself for rejection, but then, finally, she smiled again.

'Yes,' she said. Yesssssssssssssssssss! I cheered inside my head. Good man, Michael. Now what? I had to come up with a plan, dates, times, even a show. God, why didn't I think this through properly? Brilliant, Michael, absolutely brilliant. Okay, stay cool. Stop hesitating. Say something, anything, before she changes her mind. Trying to appear as calm and collected as possible, I cleared my throat.

'Right, so I can come and pick you up, and we could go into town?'

In those days, that was just how it was done. You always went to a girl's house to pick her up, and without fail, you made sure she got home safely afterward. It was a matter of respect, and anything less would have been frowned upon. She nodded.

'Okay.' Her tone was relaxed, as if this was the easiest thing in the world.

'How about Friday night?' I asked.

'Great,' she replied. That was it, I had a date. I was over the moon, barely able to contain my excitement. I turned to walk away, still riding the high of the moment, when suddenly, I heard her call after me.

'Don't you want my address?'

Jaysus, Michael. I spun back around, laughing at my own stupidity.

'Ah, yeah,' I grinned. 'That'd be helpful.' She gave me her address, and we agreed to meet on Friday at six o'clock. Just as I was about to leave again, she tilted her head and smirked.

'Oh, and my name's Cathy, by the way. And yours is?' I froze. I hadn't even got her name.

I could feel my mates' eyes burning into the back of my head, waiting for me to make a show of myself again.

'It's Michael, Michael Flynn', I said quickly. My face turned red as I let out an awkward chuckle.

'Well, Michael, I'll see you on Friday,' she said.

'See you then, Cathy'. I walked back to my table, grinning like an eejit, and as soon as I sat down, the lads erupted into laughter.

'Didn't even ask her name, ya gobshite!' Joe howled, clapping me on the back. I didn't care. I had a date.

Friday came around so fast, and I was giving myself the best self-talk I could muster: *Be cool, Michael. Be yourself. Be a gentleman.* I repeated it like a mantra, on the bus to Phibsborough where she lived, heading to her house. My palms were slightly sweaty, my stomach twisting with a mix of nerves and excitement.

I took a deep breath as I arrived and walked up the steps, my heart pounding a little faster with each one. I straightened my jacket, ran a hand through my hair, and knocked on the door.

To my horror, it wasn't Cathy who answered, it was her dad.

Ah, shit.

'Hello, sir,' I said, my voice coming out a little more meekly than I had intended.

He didn't reply right away. Instead, he took his time, scanning me from head to toe, his gaze slow and deliberate, as if he were peeling back layers to see the kind of person I really was. His eyes locked onto mine, sharp and calculating, like he was searching for even the slightest hint of deception.

'You must be Michael?' he finally said, his voice low and measured.

'That's right, sir. I'm here to take Cathy out. We're going to watch a film.'

His expression didn't change. 'What film?'

'*Bonnie and Clyde*. It's meant to be really good,' I said, a little too enthusiastically, hoping he'd believe that my main motivation for this evening was purely cinematic appreciation and not his daughter.

He paused for a moment, then gave a small nod. 'All right. Well, I hope you enjoy the film. Just make sure you bring her back safely and at a reasonable time.'

'Yes, sir,' I replied, my voice steadier this time.

Before the tension could stretch any longer, Cathy suddenly appeared in the doorway. She wore a beautiful blue dress, looking like she had just stepped out of a classic film herself.

Thank God, I thought, exhaling slightly. At least meeting her father had taken away some of the nerves about meeting Cathy.

As we sat in the dim glow of the cinema, I could hardly focus on the film. The screen flickered in front of me, but it barely registered. All I kept thinking was, *I can't believe she's here with me.* Cathy was so effortlessly beautiful, yet she didn't seem to realise it. There was no trace of vanity in her, just warmth and an easy-going charm. She was very friendly and spoke to everyone. There was no snobbery within her.

You'd expect a girl like her to know she was it, to carry herself with the confidence of someone who turns heads, but she wasn't like that at all. She was grounded, genuine, and so easy to talk to.

I kept stealing glances at her, trying not to stare. Every now and then, our eyes would meet, and I'd flash her an awkward smile before quickly looking back at the screen, pretending to be engrossed in the movie. But who was I kidding? I had no idea what was happening in *Bonnie and Clyde.*

After the movie, we caught the bus back to her house. The journey back was quiet, but not in an awkward way, just a comfortable silence between us. When we reached her house, I walked her to the door, my heart pounding a little harder when I spotted her father looming from the window. *No pressure, Michael. Just act normal.*

She smiled and said, 'Let's meet again next week in Switzer's.'

I nodded, trying to sound casual, though inside, I was over the moon. 'Yeah ... Well, I'm there most days after school.'

'Great,' she said. 'I'll see you in Switzer's.'

'Sure, see you then.'

She hesitated for a second, then added, 'And thanks for a great night.'

I grinned. 'Bye, Cathy.'

'Bye, Mick.'

She stepped inside, and I turned away, setting off on my long walk home from Phibsborough back to Pearse Street. I wanted to walk because I wanted time to play the evening over in my head. I was walking on air. Yeah. I had it bad, but times were different then. *We* were different then.

Have things changed for the better? I don't know. As Barbra Streisand sang, 'Can it be that it was all so simple then, or has time rewritten every line?' But it was simple then. We knew our place, we had a code of conduct to follow, and we followed it. I still do. Maybe that makes me sound like a dinosaur, but I believe a man should be a gentleman. It's about making sure a lady gets home safely, about courting before intimacy, to build trust and respect in a relationship. Although there were times in my life that I'm not proud of to this day; when, like all of us, I went off the rails a bit and wasn't always the best version of myself.

From that moment on, my mind was consumed with thoughts of Cathy. Every school day felt like an eternity because all I could think about was getting to Switzer's, knowing she'd be there. She became everything. Seeing her was the highlight of my week. I know I've already said how beautiful she was, but when she walked into a room, everything stopped.

I could hardly believe that she wanted to see me. It felt unreal. The time after our first date we met again in Switzer's, and she brought her friend Étaín along who, as it turned out, ended up dating my mate Joe. The four of us became insep-arable, always off doing mad things together.

As time passed, Cathy and I grew closer and closer. We spent most of our time at dances, the cinema, Switzer's, and then Moulin Rouge, which was the new hot spot in Dublin where everyone went.

I always loved going to dances. I loved the music, the energy, the excitement, and most of all, I loved dancing with the girls. Those nights were full of fun, freedom and a sense that anything was possible. Even though music was such a huge part of my life, funnily enough I never actually bought an LP. In fact, the only single I ever purchased was Elvis Presley's 'Return to Sender'. I was a massive Elvis fan.

The night Elvis died is etched in my memory. It was 16 August 1977. My friends and I were at a dance at the Stillorgan Park Hotel, a place we often went to back then. I remember it like it was yesterday. 'Pretty Flamingo' was playing, another one of my all-time favourites. The night had been full of craic, sweat and broken dreams, until the DJ suddenly stopped the record mid-song. He came on the microphone and announced that Elvis Presley had passed away.

The entire place fell into stunned silence. You could feel the shock ripple through the room. Elvis wasn't just a musician; he was a symbol of youth, rebellion and self-expression. He had been such a constant presence in all our lives that it felt almost impossible to imagine a world without him.

His death marked the end of an era. For so many of us, Elvis was the one who opened the door to a new way of being, a way where young men could express themselves more freely. He made it okay for us to be a little more colourful in our appearance, a little more flamboyant, a little more confident in who we were. Music gave us that freedom, and Elvis embodied it.

When he died, it felt like a piece of our own youth died with him. He represented the start of something special for our generation, a time when music, dance and style gave us permission to step outside the old boundaries and be ourselves. Losing him was more than losing a star; it was like saying goodbye to a part of our youth and who we were.

Another one of my favourite bands was The Monkees. Every Monday night, I'd rush home from school just in time for us all to gather as a family and watch their show together. I absolutely loved it from the very first note of the opening theme: 'Hey, hey, we're The Monkees!' The sheer joy and fun they portrayed was infectious. It was bright, energetic and full of life. I've always been drawn to the joyousness of life and joyous people. The Monkees invoked that spirit perfectly.

And of course, like everyone else at the time, I absolutely loved The Beatles. The whole world did. I'll never forget the time I saw them perform live at the Adelphi Cinema on Abbey Street. Oh my God, Dublin was absolutely hysterical that night. The excitement in the air was like nothing I'd ever felt before. Girls were screaming, people were crying and the energy was electric. It was pure madness in the best way possible.

That Beatles concert remains the only proper gig I've ever attended. Sure, I've been to countless discos, parties, and dance nights over the years, but as for live concerts, that night with The Beatles was my first and my last. And honestly, it was so incredible, it felt like it was enough. After seeing the greatest band of all time live, how could anything else compare?

The Beatles' influence was everywhere. We all embraced the look, the long hair, the flared trousers, the whole style. I have my long hair to this day, and I take great pride in it as everyone who knows me knows. I don't get touchy about most things, but my hair, I do. Over the years, people have often asked me if I'd ever chop it off for charity, but I always say the same thing: I'd rather just donate the money. Nobody's getting near my locks! That's something I'm very stubborn about. Hands off the hair!

Looking back, it was such a special time. Whenever I think of those days, I'm flooded with nostalgia. Life was vibrant, colourful and full of hope. Back then, people often said I looked like Peter Noone from Herman's Hermits. I had long hair, a big smile and prominent teeth, so I suppose I could see the resemblance myself. And of course, Peter Noone was a good-looking man, so I always took it as a compliment.

My unique look has done me no harm and is something I am very grateful for. I was aware I had a slightly different look, and honestly, I think that helped me stand out a little, especially with the ladies. But back then, there was really only one girl who ever mattered to me: Cathy. Stealing a few moments with her in the middle of all the dancing, singing and madness, that was the real magic.

But finding time alone was nearly impossible. She lived with her parents, who were always around, and coming back to mine wasn't an option as our house was already bursting at the seams. Privacy was a luxury we just didn't have.

So, romance? Well, it wasn't exactly candlelit dinners and love songs. Kissing and hugging down dimly lit alleyways, stealing brief moments wherever we could, that's just how it was for all of us back then. Hiding in the shadows, taking whatever little bit of affection we could get along with the rest of Dublin. Sometimes there would be a row of couples after dances necking down alleyways – it was the only place we had.

Cathy became such a big part of my life. Over time, she got to know my family. My mother adored her and she treated Cathy like a third daughter. My sisters worshipped her too. To them, she wasn't just my girlfriend; she was practically another sister. She was so stylish, so effortlessly cool. They looked up to her, and I did too.

It was getting close to leaving school, and we were all buzzing at the thought of leaving the priests behind and finally getting a real taste of freedom. You could smell the independence in the air, the sweet scent of doing whatever we pleased. I was delighted, and Joe was too. The pair of us finished top of the class, not bad considering all our extracurricular activities. Everyone was as shocked as we were, but feck it, we pulled it off somehow.

On the last day of school, we were practically clawing at the gates, desperate to break free. That place, those walls, those corridors echoing with the droning voices of Brothers who ruled with fear, it was behind us now. Forever. No more being strapped, no more being made to feel small. What they called discipline, we now recognised for what it was: psychotic abuse and control. But as we stepped out, something shifted. The weight that had pressed on our shoulders for years lifted, replaced by something electric, freedom.

The air felt different that day. Lighter. Charged. We were all drunk on the sheer joy of escape. By the time we made it to Schooners, it was heaving with bodies, the place alive with laughter and celebration. You couldn't move, couldn't hear yourself think over the roar of voices, everyone revelling in relief.

I was on my way. The most beautiful girl in town was on my arm, her hand warm in mine. We were ready – ready to make our way in the world and to run fast from the strict gaze of the Christian Brothers.

To mark the occasion of leaving school, we took our two ladies out to Jury's Hotel to celebrate. We thought we were very sophisticated, bringing these gorgeous girls to such a posh place. We sat there, feeling like high society, ordering coffee and tomato sandwiches. In reality, that was all we could afford, but in our minds, we had arrived. I still laugh when I think about those sandwiches, just slices of bread with soggy tomatoes. Not exactly fine dining. But we didn't care. We were young, we were in love, and we were growing up. Sitting in Jury's, sipping coffee, with our girlfriends by our sides, we felt like men.

Cathy and I became quite the couple; we were always together. It wasn't Romeo and Juliet, it was Mick and Cathy. And honestly? Romeo and Juliet had nothing on us.

She was always there for me. Through every trial and tribulation, she stood by my side. She was amazing. She was everything. And at that time, I truly believed she'd be the one forever.

Chapter 4

Man about Town

After I left school I began to spread my wings and embrace the taste of independence. So much so that I decided to set up my own little weekend stall at the Dandelion Market. Back then, it was Dublin's beating heart of creativity and counterculture. It was an open-air market unlike any other, and at the time, it was the talk of the town. The air was filled with energy and colour, and the people who came to roam its narrow lanes were just as lively and diverse as the goods on display.

The Dandelion Market wasn't just a place to shop; it was a gathering ground for artists, musicians, students and all kinds of free spirits. You could find yourself talking to a local painter, a hippie playing a guitar, a group of students debating philosophy, and a performer doing an impromptu dance. It had a bohemian, almost magical feel to it, there was always music playing, voices laughing, and the irresistible hum of life happening all around. My sister Catherine was absolutely enchanted by the place and helped me on the stall. She loved it for the characters it attracted, each one a story waiting to be told.

The market was a paradise for anyone who loved variety and creativity. Stalls were packed with treasures – from second-hand clothing that told stories of years gone by to antiques with the charm of forgotten times. There were stacks of vinyl records, glistening jewellery, perfume bottles with exotic scents, and an eclectic mix of house goods, arts and crafts. The assortment was endless, and it was all incredibly vibrant with bright colours, eclectic designs and textures. It was more than just shopping; it was a chance to explore, to get lost in the uniqueness of it all.

Looking back, those were some of the happiest days of my life. I felt as though I had truly found my calling. The hustle and bustle of the market, the excitement of people coming and going, bargaining and chatting, felt like home. I loved the interaction with everyone who came through the market, whether they were browsing or buying. I quickly became known as the person who could find whatever you needed, no matter how obscure. From jewellery to bathroom accessories, I could get my hands on it. If someone needed something, I'd already have a contact in mind, and with a smile, I'd make sure they got it. The thrill of the trade, the joy of connecting with people, just felt right.

The Dandelion Market was more than just a market; it was a melting pot of cultures, ideas and experiences. In many ways, it was the beginning of Dublin's evolution into a more multicultural city, as it welcomed new influences, new ways of thinking, and new people into the fold. It was a time when Dublin began to open its arms to the world, and the Dandelion Market stood as a vibrant testament to that change. It wasn't just a marketplace, it was a reflection of the pulse of a city that was slowly, but surely, becoming something much bigger than it had been. And for me, it was a time of discovery, excitement and endless possibility.

I was making great money on the Market. Selling was natural to me, it was in my blood. I had a way with people, a knack for persuasion, and, if I'm being honest, my looks didn't hurt either. I was young, confident and thriving. Business was so good that I could afford something that up to then I had only dreamed of owning: a car.

Not just any car, but a beautiful little grey Mini. Sleek, compact and full of character. The registration number was CZU 221. I can't remember my own phone number now, but I remember that as clear as day. That Mini was my pride and joy. I was over the moon, feeling like a proper man about town. And, as they say, a car does seem to attract more attention. Suddenly, I noticed more glances, more smiles. But none of that mattered, because there was only one girl in my life: Cathy.

Beyond the personal joy it brought me, the Mini also turned out to be a blessing for my family. Things weren't going well for the family business at the time. The biggest problem was that large stores like Dunnes Stores and Penneys had opened in the city centre, and we were probably the last drapery business left in Dublin. Once those big shops arrived, people started going into town to buy what they needed instead of supporting small, independent drapery stores like ours.

Pearse Street was close to the city, which saved us a little. But new shopping centres were opening all over Dublin, filled with well-known brands. That only made things worse for us. One by one, the other independent drapery stores shut down, they just couldn't compete. We were one of the last ones left, holding on as best we could.

With the business struggling, the debt my grandfather had left behind weighed on us. My dad had no choice but to sell his Morris Minor. Since he lived above his work, he didn't need a car that much. But on the occasions he did, my Mini was there for him. Yet no matter how hard we worked, it felt like we were only sinking further into debt. Even the wholesalers were going under. It was all just getting harder and harder, and there didn't seem to be a way out.

By then, though, something much more serious was weighing on my mind. Dad had emphysema and it was starting to get worse. I could see it in the way he moved, the way he breathed and that harsh, relentless cough, especially in the mornings, I felt for him every time. Yet, no matter how sick he was, he never once complained. He was still smoking though, it was what everyone did back then, barely giving it a second thought. Cigarettes were just a part of life. But I could see the toll it was taking. For the first time, I started to really worry about him.

While the Dandelion Market felt like home to me, it was only a weekend gig. I enjoyed it, but I needed something more, something stable, as my father put it. I think the ups and downs of his own life made him determined to guide his children towards a more secure and conventional path.

I always had a sense of my place in society. Growing up as a Pearse Street boy, I understood that getting into UCD or Trinity was unlikely. Some of my friends were choosing a different path, securing jobs in the bank. It seemed like the logical option, a stable and respectable career. Joe Byrne became a businessman. Mal joined his family's off-licence business. Joe Landy, who grew up surrounded by fields and livestock, naturally followed his roots into farming. And Barry pursued architecture. We were all workers, hard workers. It was just in our nature.

I was submitting applications to the banks, but as soon as they saw my address, my applications were disregarded. The stigma of being from Pearse Street meant facing discrimination at every turn, even when seeking employment. I didn't even get a single interview.

One day, I decided to take a different approach. I dressed the part. Mary did my hair, I put on a crisp shirt and suit, and I walked straight into the Royal Trust. My heart pounded as I made my way to 53 Dawson Street, but I convinced myself that if they met me in person, they might see beyond my address. If they could hear me speak, see my determination, they might change their minds. They might realise I wasn't a troublemaker just because I came from Pearse Street.

As I stepped into the Royal Trust, I was introduced to a man named Brian Doyle. His authority was clear from the first moment I saw him. He was tall and well-groomed, with an undeniable presence. Despite his commanding appearance, there was a warmth about him; he was friendly, approachable, and carried himself with dignity.

Unlike the typical image of a banker, he was remarkably human in his interactions. He spoke eloquently, choosing his words with care, and there was no mistaking that he was a man of importance. His confidence wasn't intimidating but rather reassuring, making those around him feel at ease. I told him about my qualifications, my strong Leaving Cert results, and my eagerness to work.

To my surprise, he was incredibly welcoming. Instead of dismissing me like the others, he listened. He offered me valuable advice and even helped me submit an application for a position at the Royal Trust. He didn't judge me or look down on me, he simply saw a young man willing to work hard. I think he took an instant liking to me, and before long, I was offered a job at the Royal Trust.

Michael Flynn

My parents were overjoyed, as was the rest of my family. A banking job was a big deal, especially for a Pearse Street boy. That job became my life for a few years. During the weekdays, I worked at the bank, and on weekends, I sold goods at the Dandelion Market with my sister, Catherine. There were a good few afternoons when I'd find myself talking to Paul Hewson, aka Bono, while he busked with his band on the entrance to the Market, never realising that the young man with the guitar would go on to become a global superstar. We exchanged fleeting words, but at the time, he was just another friendly face in the crowd, and the magic of what lay ahead was still a distant dream. But there was something about those moments, about the raw, unpolished energy of those early days that felt special, even then.

So for me, it wasn't just another responsibility: I enjoyed it and I also enjoyed the extra income. I was making good money, enough to help my parents while still lending a hand at the shop whenever I could.

After leaving school, my friends and I naturally drifted apart. We had different jobs and different schedules, and though we still saw each other from time to time, it was never like before. Meanwhile, things at home were becoming more demanding. My father's health was deteriorating rapidly, and my mother was taking on more responsibilities at the shop. I did everything I could to support them and keep things running smoothly.

I always felt a deep sense of responsibility, especially for my younger siblings, Brian, Mary and Catherine. I was making a bit of extra cash, so I decided to buy a caravan, a real clapped-out thing, barely holding together. It was on its last legs when I got it, but for just a few quid, it felt like a bargain.

It was parked in Rush, and I figured it would make the perfect little escape.

Brian, Mary, Catherine and I would head there for a few days at a time. The caravan was tiny, practically falling apart, with barely enough space to sleep. There weren't real beds, just a pull-out sofa and an old mattress, but we crammed in anyway. It was uncomfortable, a bit ridiculous, but somehow it was brilliant.

Some of my friends were around Rush at the time, so we'd meet up, go drinking and leave all the chaos of Pearse Street behind. We'd eat fish and chips, treat ourselves to Mr Whippy ice creams, and take a dip in the sea. The people there were warm and welcoming, you could feel the sense of community. In that little beaten-up caravan, I often felt more at home than I did back in the city.

My brother and sisters loved it. They couldn't wait until I had a spare day or two to take them. The best part? It was always there, waiting for us, free to use whenever we wanted. Rush South Beach became a place filled with happy memories. And looking back, that was when I first realised, I was becoming the main caretaker of the family.

Those were some of our happiest times together. Yet, I carried a weight on my shoulders, feeling like it was all up to me. If something went wrong, if there were money problems, it was my burden to bear. My father's condition grew so severe he could no longer manage the stairs, and he became confined to the living room. My mother became his primary caregiver while trying to keep the shop afloat.

Despite the mounting stress, I worked hard and tried to enjoy life where I could. Cathy was my greatest source of strength, the light at the end of the tunnel. She understood the challenges I faced, and I think her parents were pleased that I got a stable job in the bank. It meant security, a steady income and the potential to build a future.

We never explicitly talked about the future, but I believed we both knew we were meant to be together forever. In my mind, I was already planning it, I saw us buying a home, settling down, and me working my way up to bank manager. That was the life I envisioned, the life I was working towards, even as the weight of responsibility threatened to pull me under.

Chapter 5

When the Pillar Falls

It was 1970, and Dublin was changing before my eyes. The cityscape was shifting, big stores were opening, bringing excitement for some and devastation for others. But the greatest change wasn't in the streets, it was in my own home.

My father was getting worse. His breathing had become laboured, each gasp rattling through the house. The mornings were the worst. His deep, hacking cough echoed through the walls, relentless, unyielding. His emphysema was tightening its grip on him, yet no matter how sick he became, he refused to stop working. He pushed through every struggle, every wheeze, until one day, he simply couldn't. I think, in a way, he had given all he had left to give.

I remember coming home and finding him slumped in his chair, barely able to breathe. His face was pale, his chest rising and falling in a desperate effort to keep going. I had no choice, I took him straight to Sir Patrick Dun's Hospital with my mother by my side. The moment we arrived, they admitted him without hesitation. They could see how bad he was.

He was such a kind, gentle man. He never complained, never raged against his fate. It was as if he had accepted what was coming. The pain had become unbearable, chronic and constant. Maybe, deep down, he was ready to let go.

That night, as I sat by his hospital bed, he pulled me close, his voice barely more than a whisper in my ear. 'Son, would you ever get your auld da a drop of whiskey?'

I swallowed hard. 'Da,' I said softly, 'you can't drink in your condition. You know what the doctor said. How about a nice cup of tea instead?' The look in his eyes when I refused him broke my heart. He gave me a weak push, turning his head away, hurt by the only answer I could give.

The next morning, the phone rang. The hospital needed us to come immediately. My heart dropped. I turned to my mother, but she couldn't do it. The weight of it all was too much. She took my hand and whispered softly, 'Son, you go,' her eyes welling up with tears like she was already lost in grief, unable to bear the final goodbye. Her hands trembled, her voice was so soft, so sad.

I nodded. 'Okay, Mam.' I rushed to the hospital alone, but I was too late. He was already gone. I never got to say goodbye. And among all of my regrets, one of the biggest is that I never got him that drop of whiskey.

I packed up his things, the flat cap he always wore, the cigarettes he could never put down and placed them carefully into a plastic bag. My heart felt heavier with every step as I made my way home. When I walked through the door, I didn't have to say a word. My mother took one look at me and she just knew. She sat down, silent for a long time, until finally, she spoke.

'Was it peaceful, son?'

I didn't know. I hadn't made it in time. But the nurses assured me it was gentle, that he didn't suffer in those final moments. I told her what they said, hoping it would bring her some comfort.

That was the moment when everything changed.

I organised the funeral, I made sure everything was sorted – I went to the undertakers to make sure that it was properly done and as he would have wished. The weight of responsibility settled on my shoulders, and I understood, with absolute certainty, that my life had shifted in a way that could never be undone. I wasn't just a good brother any more. I was the provider, the caretaker, the man of the house.

We held a large funeral for my father. He was well-loved, both within our family and in the community. People respected him, and it showed in the turnout. We held the funeral at the church on City Quay, where my father had first seen and met my mother, from where their life together began, and now we were bringing him back there for the final farewell. I had served here as an altar boy. I knew many of the people there, which made things a little easier, though nothing could ease the weight of the day.

It was a beautiful service. The church was packed, and the crowd spilled out onto the street. Seeing so many people there, paying their respects, brought some comfort to my mother and my siblings. But grief doesn't leave with the mourners, it lingers. And for my mother, it was nearly unbearable.

She was never the same after he died. You could see it in her face, in the way she moved through the house as if she were lost. Pearse Street, once filled with memories of my father, now felt haunted by them. And the area itself was changing, crime was creeping in, making it rougher than before. It was as if everything she knew was slipping away all at once.

On top of that, she still had to care for her mother-in-law Ellen, who was growing frailer by the day. But looking after

Ellen wasn't done out of love, it was duty, obligation. None of us liked Nanny Ellen. She was a cruel woman, bitter and mean-spirited, and she made it no secret that she hated us.

I know it sounds awful to say, but part of us silently wished it had been her who passed instead of my father. My sister Catherine, never one to mince words, used to call her a horrible old bitch. And honestly, she wasn't wrong. But regardless of how we felt, my mother had to care for her, and it only added to the weight she was already carrying.

For me, my priority was simple, I had to step up. I had to help my mother and take care of my younger brother and two sisters. There were practical matters to deal with as well. I had to transfer everything into my mother's name, sort out my father's finances, and go to the banks he owed money to. I was only 19, barely an adult myself, but I had to walk into those banks and face down the managers like a man twice my age.

One meeting in particular stands out. It was at a bank on O'Connell Street. I still remember the manager, a real stuck-up bastard, the kind of man who looked down his nose at you the second you walked in. Cold, dismissive and uninterested in helping, a typical banker of the time.

I sat across from him, going through the details of my father's debts, explaining our situation, hoping for some understanding. But it was clear from the start that this fella had no sympathy. When it became obvious that he wasn't going to do anything for us, I stood up, looked him dead in the eye, and said, 'Look, we don't have the money to pay you. Do what you like.' Then I turned on my heel and walked out.

That same day it felt like everything was closing in on me. I was overwhelmed, burdened by our debts and constantly worried about my mother. I kept asking myself, *how am I supposed to carry all of this on my own?*

Whenever I feel completely swamped, I tend to step away from everything and everyone just to breathe, to clear my head. Back then, I used to smoke John Player Blue. That day, I was smoking like a chimney. I stepped outside the shop for a moment and lit a cigarette, hoping it would give me a bit of peace and maybe even inspiration.

As I stood there, taking slow drags, my eyes drifted across the street. That's when I saw him, an elderly man. His clothes were worn and hanging off him. He looked utterly alone. Something about him stopped me in my tracks. I felt it deep in my chest.

I walked across the road and gently said, 'Hello.'

When I looked down, I noticed he had no shoes on. Just bare feet, dirty, cracked, and bleeding in places. My heart broke a little right then. It made me pause and think: no matter how hard things seemed for me, at least I had shoes on my feet, a roof over my head, and something to eat. So, without thinking too much, I took my shoes off and handed them to him. His gratitude humbled me – he was so thankful for something that most of us don't even think about. That expression of gratitude, it stayed with me. He didn't complain, even though his feet must have been in pain. He simply slipped the shoes on, looked up, and thanked me softly.

We spoke for a short while. He told me he was wandering around town, trying to find somewhere safe to stay for the night. I didn't have much to spare, but I gave him a few quid anyway. It wasn't a lot, but it was something. That moment changed me. It opened my eyes. No matter how heavy life feels, or how little you think you have, someone out there is facing something even harder. I walked back across the road in only my socks. My sister Mary looked at me, puzzled, and asked, 'Mick, where are your shoes?'

I told her, 'I gave them to someone who needed them more.'

It's moments like that, simple, human moments that remind you: no matter how little you have, there is always a way to give. Even the smallest act of kindness can mean the world to someone else.

It took us a long time to adjust to life without my father. The loss wasn't just emotional, it was the absence of him in every little thing. Especially for my mother. There were so many things I never got to do with him. I would have loved to go to the pub with him, just the two of us, to sit over a pint and talk, not just as father and son, but as men, as friends. That's what saddens me the most. The missed time. The things we never got to do. The conversations we never got to have as men.

And no matter how much time passes, I still feel the loss of times that should have been.

For years after Dad's death, my life was nothing but work. Weekdays, I was in the bank. Weekends, I was at the Dandelion Market. And in whatever spare time I had left, I was helping Mam in the shop. The pressure was relentless, grief sat heavy on my chest, but I didn't have time to stop and feel it. I just kept going, because what else could I do?

But through it all, there was one thing, one person that made everything bearable. Cathy. She was my light in the dark, the one thing that brought me comfort when nothing else did. Cathy stood beside me at my father's funeral, held my hand when I thought I would break, and never once let go, no matter how lost I felt. She was my safe place, my home.

Until the night everything fell apart.

We had gone bowling. It had seemed just like any other night between us. I thought we were happy. I had no idea anything was wrong. Afterwards, we sat in the car, laughing about the game, just like always. And then, out of nowhere, she said, 'Mick, I have something to tell you.' Something in her voice made my stomach drop. The silence that followed felt like a lifetime. And then, she said it.

'Mick, I'm sorry, but I'm going to have to end our relationship.' She told me she'd met a doctor and that it was serious. She also said her parents thought it would be a great match and that it was the best thing for everyone.

The words didn't make sense. They hung in the air, unreal, impossible. I couldn't breathe. My whole world, the one steady thing I had, was shattering right in front of me. Cathy was leaving me. I begged her not to go. I pleaded, 'Please, don't do this. Please, tell me what I can do to fix it.' But she had already made up her mind – I could see it in her eyes.

Maybe I had been blind or I had been so caught up in work, in trying to hold everything together, that I had let *us* slip away. But I thought we were fine. I thought we were sailing along just as we always had. I thought she knew how much I loved her.

I found out, years later, that she had spoken to my mate Joe Byrne at Mal Deveney's wedding. She had confided in him, told him she was unsure about our future. That she didn't know if things were going anywhere. That she wanted me to take the next step and ask her to marry me.

I had no idea. She had been waiting for me, hoping I would see what she needed, what she wanted. But I was too caught up in everything else going on in my life. And Joe, loyal as he was, never betrayed her confidence. If only I had known, but it was too late.

That night, I drove her home, my hands shaking on the wheel, my vision blurred by tears. When we got to her parents' house, she stepped out of the car, hesitated for a moment, then walked up the stairs. I watched her go, knowing it was over. I gave her one last wave, and then she was gone.

I barely made it home. My heart felt like it had been ripped out of my chest. My family had never seen me like that before: silent, withdrawn, shattered. I carried that heartbreak for a long, long time. It was the first real loss I had felt since Dad died. And in some ways, it hurt even more. Years passed. Life moved on. But I never forgot her.

Then, many years later, I got a message. Cathy was sick. Very sick. And a week before she passed, she called me. Her voice was weak, but I could still hear that same warmth, the same familiarity that once made me feel so safe.

'Mick,' she said, 'I just want you to know that I never stopped loving you.' It took everything in me not to break down right then and there.

'I never stopped loving you either.' And that was it. That was our goodbye.

I lost her twice. But she was my first love. And I will always look back on our time together with great fondness.

Chapter 6

Picking up the Pieces

Chapter 6

Picking up the Pieces

The next chapter was a long and painful journey of trying to put the shattered pieces of my life back together, of desperately searching for a sense of normality in the wake of losing both my father and Cathy. The weight of grief pressed down on me, but I had little choice but to keep moving forward.

I threw myself into work, hoping that if I stayed busy enough, I wouldn't have time to feel the ache in my chest. During the week, I buried myself in my job at the bank, and on weekends, I worked in the market. My hands were permanently occupied, and my mind was distracted just enough to get by. Whenever I had any spare time, I helped out at the shop, pouring whatever energy I had left into its upkeep. It wasn't so much that I wanted to work; I *needed* to. If I stopped, even for a moment, the silence would creep in, and with it, the memories, the loneliness, the unbearable loss.

But I wasn't just working myself to exhaustion. I was also partying. A lot. Any chance I got, I was out, surrounding myself with noise, with people, with laughter that never quite reached my heart. I told myself I was having fun, and in a way, I was. It was an escape, however temporary. I drank, I danced, I laughed, anything to forget, anything to fill the emptiness.

I started dating, too. That was a strange, new experience. I had been with Cathy from such a young age that I had never really explored the dating scene before. At first, it was exciting. I met different women, went out on dates and experienced new things. But no matter how much I tried to lose myself in the moment, in the warmth of someone new, there was always that cold, lingering truth in the back of my mind: it wasn't Cathy. No one was. No one could be. I tried to convince myself otherwise, but deep down, I knew. Every smile, every conversation, every touch was a shadow of what I had once known, what I had once loved so deeply and lost.

Meanwhile, things at home kept moving forward, though I could see the toll life was taking on my mother. She was getting older, growing more tired, the weight of years and hardships becoming evident. But then, we received unexpected news, news that, though it felt terrible to admit, brought a quiet, almost shameful relief.

Ellen, our family's long-time tormentor, was very ill. She had gone away to be with her family in Roscommon, and word came back that she was on her last legs. And as awful as it may sound, we weren't exactly devastated.

She had been such a cruel woman, her presence in our lives like a dark cloud that never lifted. She was strict to the point of cruelty, always criticising, always comparing us to other children in the family, always making us feel like we were in the way. She had a way of making us feel small, unwanted, like we didn't truly belong. And now, knowing that soon she would be gone, we couldn't help but feel a certain lightness, as if a suffocating weight was finally being lifted from our chests.

When she finally passed away in Roscommon, we travelled down for the funeral. But to be honest, none of us were grieving. The most pressing concern in our household was whether my sister Catherine would still be able to have her 15th birthday party, which fell in the same week as the funeral. We weren't mourning her, we were simply waiting for this chapter to close so we could move on with our lives.

And once she was gone, something in our home shifted. It felt lighter, freer. For the first time in as long as I could remember, we had our living room to ourselves. There were no more sharp eyes watching our every move, no more judgemental comments slicing through our conversations, and no more oppressive presence making us feel like intruders in our own home. The house, at last, felt like *ours*.

But most importantly, I saw the change in my mother. A quiet relief settled over her, a tension she had carried for so long finally melting away. She seemed just a little more at peace, as if she could finally breathe without fear of criticism or scorn. And in that moment, I knew, we had all been freed from her shadow. We could finally move forward, unburdened, reclaiming our home, our lives, our happiness. So much so, I overheard my sister Mary singing 'Ding dong, the witch is dead, dry your eyes, get out of bed'.

It wasn't just the joy that we felt. It was something quieter, something deeper. A sense of peace that had been absent for far too long.

As the mid-1970s rolled in, so did a new love in my life, one that gleamed in the brightest yellow and purred like a dream. I had bought myself a brand-new Fiat 128, and from the moment I slid behind the wheel, it became my pride and joy. You could see me coming from miles away, that canary-coloured beauty turning heads everywhere I went. I didn't mind, not one bit. In fact, I relished the attention. I had always loved standing out, and this car made sure I did.

With the arrival of my Fiat, I bade farewell to my old Mini, a small sacrifice for a much flashier ride. But cars weren't the only new thing in my life. A few years after Cathy had left me, I met someone else, Jean.

I first laid eyes on her in 1979 in the Horse Show House Pub in Ballsbridge, and she was breathtaking. She had long, flowing dark hair and an effortless elegance about her. From the moment we spoke, we clicked. It was instant, easy and natural.

Not long after, Jean and I started seeing each other regularly. The more time we spent together, the closer we became. But what I hadn't realised, what caught me completely off guard, was just how well-off her family was. They weren't just comfortable; they were cinema people. They owned multiple theatres all across Dublin, including the Green Cinema, next to the Dandelion Market, the Ambassador, and several others. When she casually dropped that into conversation, I was stunned and impressed.

Then came the day she invited me to her family home in Rathmines. As I stood in front of that grand house, my stomach tightened. It was enormous. Long, sweeping stairs led up to a towering front door, and beyond the massive bay windows, I could see a lavish lounge, the kind I'd only ever glimpsed before. A sprawling garden stretched out at both the front and back, meticulously kept, so different from the narrow streets and cramped flats of Pearse Street where I had grown up.

And then I met her father. As soon as he looked at me, I knew. He could smell the inner-city kid on me, could sense the boy from the wrong side of town. His handshake was polite but cold; his smile tight, forced. He tolerated me, but

I could see it in his eyes – he disapproved of me. I wasn't what he wanted for his daughter.

But Jean? Jean didn't care. If anything, I think she enjoyed it. She got a thrill out of bringing home the working-class lad, the one her father would have never picked for her. It was rebellious. It was fun. And I was caught up in it.

Despite the tension, our relationship deepened. We ignored the side glances, the subtle jabs. Her family never came to Pearse Street, we always had to go to them. We had been together for a while, and the next natural step seemed to be asking her to marry me. Maybe, deep down, I was still reeling from the way Cathy had left. Her sudden departure had shaken me, left a scar I hadn't fully acknowledged. Perhaps I was chasing security, trying to ensure that history wouldn't repeat itself. I didn't want to be blindsided again. So maybe, in some way, proposing to Jean wasn't just about love; it was about holding onto something stable, something certain. But looking back now, I think it was just fear.

And then, one day, I asked *the* question. We were as per usual in the Horse Show House. I'd bought a ring and asked her, very casually … 'Will you marry me?'

Her response was a resounding yes but chaos wasn't far behind. Her parents were livid. My mother, on the other hand, liked Jean; she just couldn't stand the way her family looked down on us. But we didn't care. We were young, reckless and in love. At that age, you don't think about the consequences. You don't stop to second-guess yourself. You just go for it.

To prove my worth, I bought a house in Monkstown. Monkstown! And because I worked at the bank, I got a fantastic deal. I could tell, though he never said it out loud, that Jean's father was secretly impressed. For a moment, I thought maybe, just maybe, I was finally winning them over.

The invitations were sent. The arrangements were made. Everything was in place. And then, just six weeks before the wedding, it hit me: a cold, suffocating wave of panic. I *couldn't* do this.

I loved Jean, but I knew, deep down, she wasn't the one. More than that, I knew I would never be free in that world. I was already suffocating under the weight of her family's expectations. If I married Jean, I'd have to stay at the bank, play the role of the respectable banker. I'd have to pretend for the rest of my life. And I couldn't. I wouldn't.

I told my mother first.

All along, my mother had been supportive: she'd helped with the menu, the invitations and the suits, but she often quietly whispered, 'Are you sure, son? Do you really want to go ahead with this?' Maybe it was a mother's intuition or maybe she knew me better than I knew myself.

She had poured so much into the wedding, but when I finally found the words, she simply nodded. 'Okay, son.' No anger, no judgement, maybe no surprise – just under-standing.

Now I had to summon the courage to tell Jean. I took her out to the 51 Bar on Haddington Road. All evening, the words I needed to say kept looping in my mind. I wanted her to have a good night, to enjoy what would be our last date even if she didn't know it. I hoped she'd remember me kindly, not as someone who meant to hurt her. I was as gentle and attentive as I could be, but the thought kept circling around my mind on the way home, I'd have to tell her the wedding was off. The anxiety built with every hour.

Even then, I wasn't sure. Could I really do this? Could I let someone down like that? She was so excited about the wedding. It was all she talked about. And I just smiled and nodded, all the while knowing what I was about to do. It felt awful. I hate upsetting people.

As we drove back, she noticed I was quieter than usual. She asked if something was wrong. I shook my head and said I was fine. When we pulled up outside her house, the car stopped. She turned to me and said, 'Michael, I know something's wrong.' That was the moment. It was now or never.

I looked at her and said, 'Jean, I'm so sorry to do this. But I have to do what's right for both of us. I don't think I can go through with the wedding. I think it's best if we call it off.' Her face just dropped. She started to cry and I froze. I never know what to do when someone cries. I tried to explain that I never meant to hurt her, that I truly was sorry, and that I believed this was for the best. I did everything I could to make her feel better, but there was no way to soften it.

She was devastated. She jumped out of the car, slammed the door, and ran up the steps to her house wiping her tears. I felt horrible. That night, I felt ashamed and miserable. But deep down, I knew it was the right thing. Sometimes, you have to make the hard choice, even if it breaks your heart. If I'd gone through with it, I know we both would have ended up unhappy and that wouldn't have been fair to either of us.

I can imagine her father's reaction: angry that I had let his daughter down, just before the wedding, but also if I'm honest, probably happy. Relieved that his daughter wouldn't be marrying a Pearse Street boy and saying what he had thought all along – that Jean was far too good for me. Maybe he was right.

Imagining his reaction answered any lingering doubts I had about the decision I had made to call it off. Then came the aftermath, the frantic calls, the refunds, the explanations to friends and family. And, of course, the house. The beautiful house in Monkstown. I had to go back to the bank, sell it off, and repay every penny. It was a disaster. A complete mess. And yet, despite all of it, I knew I had done the right thing. For myself and for Jean.

And my friends and family knew it, too.

I had to see her one last time – there were still a few things left to settle about the house. She came to Pearse Street. And the moment I saw her, the guilt hit me like a freight train. It was written all over her face: the pain, the confusion, the heartbreak. She didn't have to say much; her silence said everything.

I tried to explain, to tell her this was the right thing for both of us, even if it didn't feel like it. My words felt hollow, even to me. Then, without drama, without anger, she reached into her pocket and handed me back the ring. Her eyes met mine, calm but shattered and in the softest voice, she said, 'Goodbye, Michael.'

And just like that, she was gone. I felt bad after that for a long time. I avoided anywhere she might be, just in case I'd run into her, as I couldn't bear the guilt and wouldn't have known what to say. I'm sure I wouldn't have been flavour of the month with her friends either.

Chapter 7

Sandymount Notions

This stage of my life? I'm calling it freedom. But as a wise man once said, 'With freedom comes great responsibility.' And let me tell you, I was about to find out exactly what that meant.

I had made up my mind. I was leaving the bank. No more suits. No more paperwork. No more pretending to care about interest rates. I was going out on my own.

I had already spoken to my mother, who had confided in me that she was exhausted: tired of Pearse Street, tired of the shop, tired of holding everything together. She needed to start taking it easy, and, as tradition dictated, it was up to the eldest son to take the reins. So, after much discussion, we agreed that everything would be signed over to me. I was to be The Man of the House. A big title but really it just meant I was about to work my backside off.

My brother Brian was more than happy to handle the accounts, probably because it meant he didn't have to lift a finger outside of crunching numbers and he had also landed a job with PMPA, the big insurance company.

I marched down to Dawson Street to tell Mr Doyle about my grand plans. He was nice enough about it, but he raised an eyebrow.

'It's a risky business, working for yourself,' he said.

'But isn't *all* business risky?' I replied. (I like to think I sounded wise, but in hindsight, I was probably just cocky.) Either way, he wished me luck, and off I went, feeling like a proper entrepreneur.

With all the big stores opening in town, our drapery business was slowly dying. No one was buying curtains or fancy fabrics from us any more because they could get them much cheaper elsewhere. On top of that, the Dandelion Market had shut down, which was a huge blow for many people. It had been a valuable source of income for the community.

Then came the construction of St Stephen's Green Shopping Centre. The arrival of all those large commercial retailers signalled the end for smaller, independent shops like ours. We were being pushed out, made obsolete.

That's when I knew we had to do something. I was wracking my brain, desperately trying to come up with a way forward, some new direction that might help us survive. And then, one day, as I was sitting outside on Pearse Street, I saw a man struggling to lug a bedside locker off a bus.

It hit me like a bolt of lightning. Why should people have to go into town for furniture? And just like that, I had the idea to sell furniture. I struck a deal with a manufacturer called Henry Ivory and started stocking furniture. People loved that they could grab a chest of drawers or any other bits for their home without trekking into the city. Business was booming.

So much so that one day, someone came in asking for a chest of drawers, and I had just sold the last one. But did I let a little thing like not having stock stop me? Absolutely not. I ran into the back, emptied out my mother's chest of drawers, and sold it on the spot. The customer was delighted.

My mother? Not so much. When she walked in and found her things dumped on the floor, she roared the house down.

'MICHAEL! Why are all my dinner mats and cutlery on the floor, and more importantly, where has my chest of drawers gone?' When she called me Michael, I knew I was in for it.

'Someone came into the shop looking for a chest of drawers, and we'd sold out. And of course, I'd never want to let a customer down. Plus, we made a few quid,' I said, trying to put a positive spin on it.

'Are you mad, Michael Flynn? What's next, selling my bed for a few extra bob?'

'Mam, it's business!'

She was having none of it. The next day, I was sent out to get her a new chest of drawers and I did as I was told. Lesson learned? Not quite. I was hooked on selling, and if something had a price tag on it or even if it didn't, I was going to flog it.

With the furniture side of things going well, I got another idea. Ergas. Everyone needed bottled gas at the time, so I became an agent, bought a van, and started delivering all over the city. I advertised wherever I could, shop windows, the radio, newspapers and word of mouth. This venture did really well. I looked the part too, rocking the oversized Filofax, flashy rings and with a John Player Blue always in hand. Even Del Boy would've been green with envy.

My sister Mary helped out, and sometimes we'd have to deliver gas to flats right at the top of a never-ending staircase. After a long day's work, I'd be hauling these massive bottles of gas up step after step, feeling like I was climbing Everest with every delivery. But it paid off. I became the number one dealer in Dublin, and before long, I had two vans on the road.

Back then, there were no mobile phones, just two-way radios. My mother would take the orders over the landline, radio them in, and off we'd go. It was like a military operation, except instead of saving lives, we were saving people from running out of gas mid-dinner.

Things were flying, so I opened another furniture shop in Ringsend. My Auntie Angela ran it, and we'd pile goods onto the footpath, which naturally led to people stopping and buying things. Encouraged by the success, I then opened a warehouse in Coolock for all the furniture. I had businesses popping up left, right and centre.

I was making money, and let me tell you, it felt good. I was becoming somebody. A proper businessman. But Pearse Street was changing. It was getting rougher, and I could tell my mother had had enough. The last straw was when one day in 1981, my sister Mary was working in the shop in Pearse Street when a fella burst through the door, knife in hand, and forced her to empty the till. She was terrified, and that was it, enough was enough.

Something had to change, but I wasn't sure what. I looked at all the businesses, examined the money coming in, and arranged a meeting with the bank. My main priority at that time was to find a beautiful home for myself, Mary and my mother.

I wanted to buy in Sandymount because my Mam's sisters, Angela and Rosemary, lived there. I knew how much it would mean to her to be close to them, especially as she was getting older. It was a better area, still close to Pearse Street but also near the sea. I waited and held out hope, and eventually, a beautiful three-bedroom house came up, in Farney Park, Sandymount, D4. It had a lovely front garden and an even more beautiful back garden. I scraped together enough for the deposit and managed to secure a mortgage. It felt like a dream come true.

I couldn't wait to tell Mam and Mary the news. I was literally hyperventilating with excitement because I knew how much this would mean to them. After years of not having a proper home and struggling, I had managed to turn it around and finally give them the house they'd always wanted and deserved. I sat Mary and my mother down and said, 'I have something to tell you.' Taking a deep breath, I continued, 'I've bought us a beautiful house in Sandymount, and we'll be moving there soon.'

The joy and pride on my mother's face were unmistakable. She was over the moon, as if she had just won the lottery. With tears in her eyes, she threw her arms around me, thanking me over and over again. Mary was just as delighted. At long last, they would be free of Pearse Street after so many years of struggle. Of course we kept the shop going but not to have to live there was a great burden lifted for my mother.

When the day to leave Pearse Street finally came, my mother took one last look around, stood at the door for a moment, then firmly closed it. She never looked back. She never set foot in the Pearse Street shop again. And I don't blame her.

At this stage, I had my shops, my warehouse, my businesses, and my beloved yellow Fiat. I was a well-known businessman, a self-made man, and I was only just getting started. Looking back, I worked my backside off for it. But I loved it. I never understood people who didn't want to work, who didn't get a thrill from making a living, from building something. To me, that was the real buzz. Providing for my family, securing their future, that was my real success.

And as for my mother? She lived the peaceful, happy life she always deserved. And that made it all worth it.

Chapter 8

Through Thick and Thin

Brian and Catherine had moved on. They both got married and settled down early enough in life. My relationship with Brian was fine. We got along well enough, but as we got older, we naturally drifted apart. We became different people, I suppose. He was quieter, more reserved, one of those people who preferred to keep himself to himself.

As kids, though, we were thick as thieves. We had a shared love for collecting things, yes, we were absolute nerds. I collected beer mats, and Brian was obsessed with stamps. The moment an envelope entered the house, he pounced on it like a cat on a mouse, tearing it open just to get at the stamp. Meanwhile, I eagerly awaited the rare occasion when Dad would return from the pub with a fresh beer mat for my collection. It didn't take much to keep us entertained in those days.

And then there was Scalextric, the holy grail of childhood entertainment. We spent hours racing those little cars around the track, shouting, arguing and laughing.

My personal favourite game, though, was Monopoly. Even back then, I had a knack for selling things, and I almost always ended up with the most properties. Brian never seemed too bothered about winning, he just rolled the dice and hoped for the best. Meanwhile, I was out there playing a real estate mogul, charging extortionate rent and driving my family into jail. Good times.

As we grew older, Brian and I still got along, but we were undeniably different. If we ever went out to a pub, I'd be the one chatting away, making friends with half the bar, while Brian would sit back quietly. I was the loud, larger-than-life one, while Brian preferred to stay in the background.

Sometimes I wonder if I overshadowed him a little. Maybe I took over too much without realising it. But it was never intentional, it was just my nature. And maybe it was part of being the eldest. That said, for someone as shy as Brian, he didn't have any trouble attracting the ladies. One particular day when he was about 18 we were in the shop. A girl he had dated for a while stormed in, absolutely sobbing. She marched straight over to Brian, threw herself onto the chair next to him, and started pouring her heart out, declaring her undying love.

Brian, ever the gentleman, tried to console her while gently letting her down. He was doing a decent job of it, too, until I glanced up and saw another girl walking into the shop. She was also in tears. Also looking for Brian. Before I could even get a word out, she spotted him … comforting another crying girl. And that was it. She stormed over, tears turning to rage. I remember thinking, *Oh, shit. You're on your own here, brother.*

The image of Brian sitting there, trapped between two sobbing women, looking like he wanted the ground to swallow him whole, is one that has stayed with me. He did his best to calm them both down before finally blurting out that he didn't want to see anybody. Which, of course, was a lie because by that point, he had already met his future wife, Mary Higgins.

Brian hated Pearse Street as much as my mother did. He was asthmatic, like my father, and the thick, smoky air of the city centre wasn't exactly ideal for his lungs. As soon as he could, he got out. He and his wife Mary got a house together, and they were very happy for many years and had children of their own.

Naturally enough, as time went on, life took us down different paths. Brian and I didn't spend as much time together as we used to. It wasn't anything dramatic or deliberate. It was just life. He got married, had three children, Owen, Sarah and Deirdre, and he built a life of his own. And I was caught up with my own responsibilities, chasing career goals, dealing with the day-to-day hustle that comes with being a business owner. We were always there for each other, but not as close, not in the way we'd been when we were younger.

But as the years passed and circumstances shifted, we slowly found our way back to each other. Especially after Brian retired from AXA, where he had worked for most of his professional life in insurance. It was then that our bond quietly began to strengthen again. I had taken on more business ventures, and without hesitation, he stepped in to help me once he had the time. And in that space, we reconnected, not just as brothers, but as friends. At one stage, we were talking every single day. About business. About life. About nothing and everything. I trusted Brian completely. There was a deep, easy comfort in our conversations.

He was a good brother. A kind man. Gentle in his way, and incredibly dependable. After retiring, he found joy in something he'd always been passionate about: woodwork. He opened up a little workshop in Coolock, not far from where I was based. It wasn't flashy or big, but it was his haven. Brian was an extremely talented craftsman. Shelves, wardrobes, tables ... you name it, he could build it. And not just build it but build it well. You could see the care in every corner and joint.

I still have a few pieces of his furniture in my house. Every time I walk past them, I think of him. There's something grounding about having that, something he made with his own hands. A quiet legacy.

But as time wore on, his health began to fade. Brian's asthma was getting progressively worse. As the years went on, it took more of a toll. He became noticeably more frail. He needed a stick to walk, and the energy he once had seemed to drain bit by bit. I worried about him. We all did. It was hard to watch someone so capable become physically diminished. Then came COVID, and that's when things really changed.

He deteriorated rapidly. We still don't know if it was COVID itself or something else that pushed him over the edge, but whatever it was, it hit him hard. He was admitted to hospital in early 2021, and because of the lockdown rules and restrictions, we weren't allowed to see him. That, I think, was one of the hardest parts. To know your brother is in a hospital bed, struggling, and you can't even be by his side …
It was unbearable.

I texted him when he was there and he replied when he could. His messages were short, but they meant everything. They were our only connection during those final days. There's something deeply unnatural about not being able to sit with someone you love when they're at their most vulnerable. Not being able to hold their hand, comfort them, say the things that matter in person. It broke our hearts.

He wasn't in hospital long. Towards the very end, they allowed Mary, his wife, and their children in to see him. I'm grateful for that, at least. They were able to say goodbye, to hold him, to give him peace in his last hours. But I wasn't there. I couldn't be. And that's something I'll always carry. That absence.

In his last days I could only text him. This is how so many people were talking to their loved ones in hospital – people they knew they would never get a chance to see again.

Not being able to see my brother in person and only being able to reach him by a WhatsApp message was so frustrating, but normal for the time, sadly. I texted him one afternoon, just a simple, 'Hi, how are you doing today?'

He replied, 'Doing ok. Had a CT scan yesterday, no clots, so that's good. No improvement, but no disimprovement either. They're going to try reducing the oxygen I need.' That was some good news at least. I kept praying and hoping he would make it through.

I checked in again later that evening, just to ask how he was. He said it had been a rough day. They wouldn't let him take the oxygen mask off and he'd had loads of needles. Said he'd talk tomorrow. The next day, he messaged first. Told me he didn't really feel sick as such just short of breath and very weak. Said the doctors reckoned he was 'holding his own' and that hopefully he'd get better. I told him to stay strong and positive, and that I'd check in again the next day.

I felt a sense of hope after receiving this. Maybe God would be kind and he would pull through. I tried to keep as positive as I could even if it was only through text. I told him that was good news, that things would keep improving. He thanked me.

I asked if he could take a call, but he said not yet. Said even if he did, I wouldn't understand him with the mask on, so there was no point. I told him I understood, and that I'd check in tomorrow.

The next day, I checked in again, hoping things had improved, but my heart sank as it was not meant to be. The last text came through from Brian. 'Thanks for everything Mick. I love you. Goodbye.' I can't describe what that felt like – when I found out that I would never see my brother again and that would be the last communication between us. I couldn't see my phone because of the tears. I managed to respond with 'Brian, I'm so sad I can't visit you. There's so much I want to say. You've been a good brother to me, and I'm going to miss your friendship. I love you. Cheers.'

That was it. The last time we spoke. Strange how something so big can be reduced to a few lines on a screen. The whole situation was insane. I will hold onto these messages forever.

When he passed, the funeral was a stripped-back, sad version of what it should have been. Brian was loved by family, friends and colleagues. Under normal circumstances, the church would have been full to the rafters. But it wasn't. Because of the restrictions, we weren't even allowed inside. We stood outside, spaced apart, trying to process the loss. Watching through the doors as the priest carried out the rites. Like something out of a weird dream, or an apocalyptic film. We couldn't sing. We couldn't speak. We couldn't even say proper prayers out loud together. Just stood there in the cold, looking in, with our hearts heavy.

He was cremated afterwards. That part was quiet too. It took a long time before we were able to properly lay his ashes to rest. Everything felt like it was on pause. That chapter in our lives, his chapter, deserved a bigger close. More people. More stories shared. More laughter, even through the tears. But we did what we could. We mourned in our own ways.

And we remembered him, not just for how he died, but for how he lived.

Brian was a good man. A loving brother. A quiet helper. A craftsman. A thinker. A kind soul. And I miss him every single day.

Out of all my siblings, Mary and I were the closest. Maybe it was by default in some ways. She never married, and we ended up living together for much longer than I did with my other siblings. She was also deeply involved in the day-to-day life of the family, helping out constantly in the shops, taking on responsibilities that others didn't have the time or capacity for. Mary and I stayed side by side for years, and that created a bond that was deep, unspoken and lasting.

We were inseparable in many ways. We worked together, lived together, laughed together, and yes, struggled together too. I knew Mary inside and out. She was my right-hand woman, my partner in crime, and the one I could always count on. I absolutely adored her. But Mary carried heavy burdens, and she had her demons.

She struggled for many years with her mental health. Depression was a constant shadow in her life and like so many people, she turned to alcohol as a way of coping with the pain. She was, by every definition, an alcoholic. But what made me proud, truly proud, was that she recognised that. She acknowledged her issues and made the decision to change. Mary stopped drinking more than 30 years before she died. That's no small feat. That takes immense strength.

But in her younger years, before she got sober, I remember vividly how heavy her drinking was. Whiskey was her drink of choice, nothing light or diluted, just the strongest stuff she could get her hands on. She'd drink it like it was water. I recall one particular night at the Horse Show House, a pub we used to go to. She was drinking her usual whiskey and the atmosphere was lively, everyone was having a great time. And then suddenly, Mary just collapsed in the middle of the pub. She was so intoxicated she couldn't stay on her feet. The whole place gathered around, concerned. We picked her up and brought her home. I think my sister Catherine helped her a lot during those darker times. Catherine was always someone Mary could confide in.

Over time, Mary sought out help. She joined Alcoholics Anonymous and took control of her life. She also spent many years on Librium, which I believe helped her manage both her anxiety and her depression. I don't know if her struggles stemmed from loneliness, unresolved grief, or just the complexities that some people are born with. But what I do know is that she faced them, she fought them and, in many ways, she won.

Mary never had many romantic relationships. She had plenty of female friendships, close ones, but not many boyfriends, and certainly nothing serious. She did, however, have a tendency to take in lonely or lost souls, people who were struggling or who didn't quite fit in elsewhere. She had a big heart, and I think she believed that by helping them, by healing others, she might be able to heal something inside herself. She was deeply empathetic like that.

My mother used to tease her, saying, 'Mary, do you know what you need? You need to find yourself a man and get pregnant.' But deep down, I think that was the last thing Mary wanted or needed. She wasn't cut from that cloth. She was her own person, independent, headstrong and a little unconventional.

As a child, she was a real character. I remember all of us being dressed up and sent off to Mass on Sundays, and Mary, like clockwork, would pretend to faint just to get out of it. She'd go down like a sack of potatoes, and we'd all scramble around her. It became her little routine. I'm pretty sure my parents knew she was faking, but they went along with it anyway. It was harmless mischief.

Though she didn't always open up to me about her innermost feelings, I knew she struggled. I could feel it. Life wasn't easy for her. But despite it all, she remained strong. She faced her challenges head-on, and I will always admire her for that. I miss her every single day. She was a big presence in my life, and her absence still feels strange.

And you know, out of all my siblings, she was the only one I ever trusted to do my hair. That probably says more than anything else about how close we were. She was complicated, kind, stubborn, funny and strong. And she was mine. My sister. My best friend. My constant. I was devastated when she told us she had lung cancer. A year after the diagnosis, she died in January, 2020, just before the world was upended by Covid. I'll never stop missing her.

Catherine, my younger sister – I've always felt this deep, natural urge to protect her. It wasn't something I ever had to think about, it just was. Especially after Dad passed away, that instinct to shield her, to keep her safe, became even stronger. I felt like it was my duty, my responsibility, to make sure she was okay. She was so young, and I knew she looked up to me. She idolised me in a way that made me feel both proud and deeply responsible. I carried that like a badge of honour.

I have such a clear memory of her, tiny little Catherine in her school uniform, hugging her teddy bear, standing outside the shop on Pearse Street, waiting patiently for me to come back. I'd be off at meetings or trying to close a deal, and there she'd be, standing like a little soldier, always looking for me. After Dad died, I think she clung to me even more. She needed someone, and I tried my best to be that someone.

Catherine and I have never had a proper argument, not once in our whole lives. The closest we ever came to having one was years later, when we'd moved Mam to Farney Park in Sandymount. Everything in the house was sorted except the washing machine, which was the one last thing we needed. While I was away, Catherine and her husband took it upon themselves to buy one for Mam.

I remember coming home and seeing the washing machine already in place. I asked where it came from, and Mam told me Catherine had sorted it. My pride took a hit, big time. I've always seen myself as the provider. That's my job. I provide. I look after the family. So yes, I'll admit, I was a bit put out.

I said to Catherine, 'That's my job. I get things for Mam.' And she just laughed and said, 'Oh for God's sake, Michael, don't be so ridiculous. Will you stop?' And that was that. A silly little moment over a washing machine, that's as close as we've ever come to falling out. But it mattered to me because being the provider has always been a big part of who I am.

I've always been the protective big brother. When Catherine was 15, she begged me to take her to a party I was going to. She really wanted to come, and after a bit of back and forth, I agreed, but with strict instructions: she had to stay by my side and not wander off.

I knew she had a crush on one of the stall holders from the Dandelion Market. He had a stall next to mine and his name was Stan. He was around 17, a bit younger than me. 'Stan the Man' we called him back then. To be honest, I was never that keen on him, but she certainly was. Sure enough, we got to the party, and before I knew it, she was chatting away to him. I kept an eye on them, just in case, but I must've looked away for a second, and when I turned back, there she was, kissing him!

That was it for me, I completely lost the plot. I was fuming. My 15-year-old sister snogging a fella in the middle of a party? Absolutely not. I marched over, took her by the arm, and got her out of there as fast as I could. She wasn't impressed, told me I was always ruining her fun and never let her do anything. But I reminded her, like any big brother would, that she was still just a kid and that I wasn't going to stand by while she got herself into trouble.

Looking back, I know it probably seemed over the top to her at the time. But that was just me doing what I've always done, watching out for her. As we got older, I think I might have rubbed off on her a bit. She went into business for herself, antiques and jewellery, her two great loves. She's always had an eye for beauty and a real knack for sales. Just like her brother. She'd go to antique fairs, find hidden gems, and resell them at a tidy profit. She was brilliant at it. And she always managed to bring in a good income to support her family. I was so proud of her.

Catherine became a devoted mother, raising a beautiful daughter and son, and now she's got lovely grandchildren too. Her health hasn't always been the best, and even though I've been up to my neck with work, I always try to be there for her when she needs me. That will never change.

Through everything – losing Brian, Mary, and then my own wife – Catherine has been a rock. She was there through the darkest times, steady and unwavering. I honestly don't know what I would've done without her. She's been more than just a sister: she's been my support, my backbone, the person I could lean on when I felt like I couldn't stand any more.

Chapter 9

My Margaret

By 1984, life was actually going quite well. I was living in Sandymount with my Mam and my sister Mary. The shops were thriving; we had a good set-up going. In fact, business was booming so much that I managed to open a second furniture shop in Ringsend. Pearse Street was flying, we were doing great, and things were moving in the right direction. Everything felt smooth, manageable and optimistic for a change.

To be honest, I was living the high life. I was enjoying myself, probably a bit too much, in hindsight. I had a bit of money in my pocket, I was single, and I was free of worry. I was doing well for myself and, well, I won't lie, I was popular with the ladies. Back then, I was a good-looking fella (if I do say so myself), and I definitely had my fair share of admirers. More than a few, in fact.

One woman in particular stands out in my memory. Her name was Jackie. We only dated for a short while, but she became obsessed with me. She started following me everywhere. I'd walk into a pub, and when I turned around, I'd spot her standing across the road or peeking around corners just to get a glimpse of me. It was a bit of a joke among my friends to start with, but it quickly became unsettling.

It wasn't quite *Baby Reindeer* levels of madness, but it was starting to veer dangerously close. She would sit in her car outside the shop for hours, just staring in through the window, watching and waiting for me to come out. She even sent flowers, on multiple occasions. The lads thought it was hilarious, but deep down, I was getting a bit freaked out. Thankfully, she eventually lost interest and moved on. Maybe her obsession went somewhere else. But my obsession was my business and growing my empire. A building had become vacant in Ringsend and had caught my eye.

At the time, I was doing well in the furniture business, but I was eager to branch out into groceries. The location of the building was ideal, surrounded by residential areas, and I thought it would be perfect for a grocery store. So, my next step was to approach the Mace organisation. I got in touch with a man named Matt Melia, who was their operations manager. He came down to view the premises, and after looking around, he agreed to let me operate under the Mace brand. They would supply all the groceries, and I would buy directly from them. We signed an agreement, and part of the deal was that the shop would carry full Mace branding. If they had a special offer, I had to make sure it was promoted in the shop. It all started off really well. The Mace branding gave the shop a solid identity, and we ended up running it successfully for about eight years. It did so well, in fact, that I decided to open another shop, this time on Pearse Street.

Around that time, a girl called Margaret started working in the Mace shop in Ringsend. She was Eddie Fitzpatrick's sister who I was long-time friends with. The Fitzpatricks were well known to us. Their scrap yard was just behind the shop on Pearse Street. We could see their place right from the bedroom window.

Margaret was a beautiful girl. She was tall, elegant and had a great sense of humour. When she came to work for me, I noticed she had a spark. She was clever, confident and maybe I'm being a bit conceited here, but I thought she was giving me the glad eye from early on.

She also happened to be great at managing my not-so-secret admirer, Jackie. Whenever Jackie came into the shop asking for me, Margaret would calmly tell her I was busy or away, then she'd ring me laughing, saying, 'She's outside again, waiting for you!' It became a running joke between us and those jokes started a fun rapport between us.

Back then, the Mace brand was quite strict about presentation. Staff had to wear navy uniforms, neat pencil skirts and matching tops. It was a different time. Ours was the first self-service supermarket in the area, so customers came in and took what they needed from the shelves themselves, instead of queuing up at the counter. It was modern, efficient and ahead of its time. Margaret was a brilliant addition to the team, always punctual and hardworking, as well as easy on the eye. As time went on, we grew closer. There was a connection between us, unspoken at first.

One day, I went upstairs to check the cigarette stock in the storeroom. As I was counting, I turned around and there she was, Margaret had followed me in. We started chatting about the day-to-day running of the shop, then out of nowhere, she leaned in and kissed me. It caught me completely off guard but in the best way. That was the first time I kissed the woman who would one day become my wife.

From then on, we started seeing each other more regularly, although at first it wasn't anything serious. I was also seeing a few other girls at the time, if I'm being honest. I was young, single and enjoying myself, living the 'man about town' life-style. Entrepreneur. Socialite. Bit of a local legend, really. If you needed something, anything, I was the guy who could sort it.

Still, Margaret and I enjoyed each other's company. We went to the pictures, went dancing, and she got on well with my family. We'd known each other's families for years and I was worried at first about how they'd react to me dating their sister. But to my surprise, they were delighted. They trusted me.

I was caught up in the high life, letting my hair down, and without realising it I'd started taking my eye off the ball. I should've been more focused on the bigger picture, but instead, I was focused on having fun. Then one day in 1985, Margaret pulled me aside and said, 'Michael, I need to talk to you.'

I knew from her tone that it was serious. My heart sank. I had a sinking feeling that I knew what she was going to say before she even opened her mouth.

'Michael,' she said, 'I'm pregnant.' My response may have not been what she was hoping for. *Shhhhhhhhhhhhhhhhhit*, I thought.

It hit me like a brick. I felt a wave of panic. I wasn't ready to be a father, nowhere near it. That kind of responsibility was the furthest thing from my mind. I was terrified. Not just about the baby, but about how my mother would react. She was a modern woman in many ways, but the idea of her son having a child outside of marriage? That was another story.

Margaret, on the other hand, seemed quietly happy and ready to embrace motherhood. She looked at me, searching for a reaction. I think she was hoping I'd propose, or at least express some joy, but I couldn't. I froze. I panicked. I mumbled something about supporting her as best I could, but my heart wasn't in it. And she could see that.

Looking back, I feel ashamed of how I handled it. I was young, foolish and selfish. I wanted to carry on like nothing had changed, hoping it might all just go away. And to make matters worse, Margaret didn't really start to show until the final month of her pregnancy. Nobody knew. Not my sisters, not my Mam, nobody. I kept that one to myself as long as possible.

That was, until Mary saw her. And she was knocked sideways. Margaret was obviously heavily pregnant and only then did she reveal that the baby was mine. Mary told Catherine, and soon enough, the news spread like wildfire. Catherine insisted that Mam had to be told. Mary agreed. I, on the other hand, was trying to stay as far out of the way as possible.

Catherine sat Mam down and told her. Mam was furious, not just because Margaret was pregnant, but because it had all been kept from her. She felt blindsided. And even though she wasn't overly religious, she had certain expectations. She wanted better for me, and this situation didn't fit into that picture.

That day, Mary forewarned me that Mam had been told; that night, as I stepped through the front door, I knew what was coming. Mam was standing there, arms crossed. She looked me dead in the eye and said, 'Michael, I hear congratulations are in order.' I didn't know what to say. I was just a boy, really. Naive. Caught off guard and full of fear. So, I plastered on a smile and said, 'I know, isn't it brilliant? I'm going to be a dad, Mam.'

She saw right through me.

She looked at me and said, 'I hope you're going to do right by her, Michael.'

I nodded. 'Yeah, yeah … of course I will, Mam.'

But the truth is, I wasn't present. Not emotionally, anyway. I hadn't come to terms with the reality of it all. And then, the day finally arrived. Margaret was taken to the hospital to give birth to our daughter, Michelle.

The night Margaret was in hospital giving birth to Michelle, I was out on a date with another woman. It's something I'm not proud of, and I feel a deep sense of regret that I wasn't there to hold Margaret's hand and welcome Michelle into the world. But I was in a different place – trying to escape reality, to forget the heartbreak and loss in my life by going out partying and losing myself in dating lots of women.

Back then, it wasn't common for men to be present in the delivery room; it just wasn't the done thing. And truthfully, I didn't want to be there. I know that might sound cold, maybe even callous, but at the time, that's simply how I felt. That was the mindset. My sister, Mary, was with Margaret throughout the birth and stayed with her through the night until Michelle was born on 24 July 1986.

A few days later, Margaret came out of hospital with Michelle and went back to her family home. I gave her a little time to settle and then I went to visit them both. The first time I held my daughter Michelle in my arms, something shifted in me. It was as if time stopped. And that was the moment everything began to change. I looked down at her tiny face, so perfect, so pure, and my heart completely melted. In that one moment, I fell deeply, unconditionally in love. I wasn't prepared for it. Nothing could have prepared me for how much love I felt. Overwhelmed doesn't even begin to describe it. I was overjoyed, and for the first time in my life, I felt something bigger than myself, something real, something grounding.

From that moment on, I knew I had to support her and Margaret, no matter what else was going on in my life. And thankfully, I wasn't alone in that. My mother and Margaret grew very close during that time. They shared a bond, two strong women who both wanted what was best for Michelle. My sisters rallied around us too, showing up with kindness, love and helping hands. Margaret would spend long days in our house, and I'd find myself over in hers. We became two families blended into one, even if things weren't exactly traditional.

Chapter 10

Bye-bye Mammy

Chapter 10

Bye-bye Mammy

The truth is, I was still a bit of a rogue back then, especially where the ladies were concerned. I was distracted, still chasing other women, still trying to live like I hadn't become a father. I took my eye off the ball, off all the balls, and that recklessness bled into the rest of my life. The shops started to suffer. Business slowed, and I wasn't paying attention the way I should have been. I'd left the wrong people in charge, and they made a complete mess of it.

With Margaret no longer working in the shops, and with me too busy being everywhere but where I needed to be, the people I trusted saw their chance. They started stealing from me, and because they were locals and knew everyone that came into the shop, they would often give groceries away for free. I was too slow to catch on. There was even a fella who was meant to buy one of the shops from me for £40,000. That sale never happened. He vanished. I was counting on that money to stay afloat.

Also, people had stopped buying gas cylinders at that point, so that was another source of income that stopped.

Those people who were stealing from me … I had been so good to them. I wasn't just a fair boss, I was kind. I treated them like family. If they needed an advance on their wages, I gave it, no questions asked. Time off? Take it. I never gave out when they made mistakes. On special occasions, I sent them home with food parcels. I made sure they were looked after.

And still they stole from me. Sometimes I think the kinder you are to people the more they take advantage, which is an awful thing to think but also an awful way to behave on their part. That betrayal, it cut deep. It wasn't about the money. It was the principle. I had shown them nothing but compassion, and they paid me back in dishonesty. That hurt.

Everything seemed to be crumbling around me. The businesses were going under. One after the other. I was drowning, and no one would throw me a rope. The banks turned their backs. Not a single offer of help. Doors I thought would open slammed shut in my face. The pressure was unbearable.

But the most foolish thing I did was put the tax man on the long finger. I wasn't keeping track of my tax, and I hadn't been accounting for everything the way I should have been. This weighed heavily on my mind and caused me huge anxiety. It got to the point where I dreaded the sound of the letterbox. That sharp, sudden flap, once such an ordinary part of daily life, had become a source of deep anxiety. I'd freeze every time I heard it, already knowing what lay waiting on the floor: final reminders, overdue payment demands, stern letters from suppliers and – worst of all – those ominous envelopes stamped with the unmistakable mark of Revenue. I'd fallen behind badly on both business and personal tax. I had let everything pile up around me until it became too much to face.

One morning, a letter came through from Revenue. This one wasn't just another reminder, it was a summons. They wanted me to attend a meeting at their office in Mount Street. I owed £10,000. Back then, that was a staggering amount of money. I remember holding the letter in my hand, feeling the panic rise in my chest like a tide I couldn't hold back. My blood pressure must have been sky-high. I'd really messed things up. The anxiety was crushing and relentless. I couldn't think straight, couldn't sleep properly.

The thought of walking into that office, of being confronted with every mistake and failure, haunted me. My mind spiralled into worst-case scenarios: prison, bankruptcy, complete ruin. That's what fear does – it distorts reality, stretches your worries into something monstrous and consuming.

Eventually, the day of the meeting came. I got up early, barely able to eat, and set off towards Mount Street. My heart pounded with every step, my thoughts raced in exhausting loops. I felt like I was walking to my own judgement day.

On my way, I saw a man approaching. He wasn't dressed like most people; he wore old trousers and had a large shawl draped loosely around his shoulders. There was something timeless about him. He didn't walk with urgency, but with a calm presence that drew my attention.

He stopped directly in front of me and said, 'Hello.' I nodded, managing a tight, uneasy smile. 'Hello.' Then he said, 'You're on your way to the Revenue, aren't you?' I froze. 'How did you know that?' He smiled gently. 'I'm just a strange man. I know these things.'

I looked down at myself, no paperwork in hand, no signs of where I was going. Nothing that could have given me away. Then he looked me directly in the eyes and said, 'Don't worry. Everything is going to be fine.'

I can't explain it, but something shifted at that moment. Like a sliver of light cutting through thick fog, his words brought with them a quiet, unexpected calm. They reached deep inside me, beyond the chaos, and settled there. I nodded slowly and thanked him before continuing on my way.

At the Revenue office, I was met by the type of civil servant you'd expect: professional, stiff and perhaps a bit too comfortable watching someone like me squirm. He reviewed my case, page by page, while I sat there sweating.

All I could do was be honest. 'I've messed up,' I told him. 'I let things get out of control. I never meant to avoid anything, I just couldn't keep up.'

He listened, took notes and, after a pause, said they'd be in touch to arrange a plan for repayment. That was it. No shouting, no accusations, no legal threats. Just a plan. A glimmer of hope. Still, the idea of trying to find £10,000 felt impossible.

When I stepped back outside, there he was again. The same man, sitting calmly on the steps across the street, as if he'd been waiting for me all along.

He looked up and called out, 'How did it go?' Slightly shocked to see him again, I crossed over and said, 'As well as it could, I suppose. But I've got a mountain of debt to climb.' He smiled again. 'Don't worry. Everything is going to be fine.'

'I hope you're right,' I said. 'I am,' he replied with certainty.

I have never forgotten that encounter. It felt spiritual, like he'd been sent from somewhere beyond, a messenger of sorts. Whether it was God, the universe, or something else entirely, I still don't know. But I felt it. In that moment, I truly believed he was connected to something greater than either of us.

I walked home not weighed down by dread, but with an odd sense of peace. My mother was in the kitchen when I arrived. She looked up and asked, 'So, how did it go, son?' I said, 'I think everything's going to be all right.'

'Why?' she asked.

'Because today … I think I spoke to God,' I replied.

She gave me that sideways look only a mother can give. 'Okay, Michael.'

But here's the strangest part of it all: the Revenue never contacted me again. Not a single letter. Not a phone call. Nothing. I still don't know what happened in that office, what changed, what was overlooked, or how things just sorted themselves out.

And I do believe there are forces at work in this world that we can't see or understand. Our perception is limited. But I believe that day, I encountered something extraordinary. Whether he was an angel, a prophet, or just a deeply intuitive soul, I'll never know. But he wished me luck that day, and I've never forgotten him.

Unfortunately that luck didn't hold.

I was sitting in the Pearse Street shop, barely managing to keep the doors open, holding everything together by the thinnest thread. I was trying to piece together some sort of plan, staring at spreadsheets that no longer made sense when Mary came into the stop, walked around the counter and sat down across from me, her face pale and serious. And before she even spoke, I knew.

'Michael,' she said gently, 'I have something to tell you.'

My heart sank like a stone. I could feel it before the words left her mouth. I just *knew* it was about Mam. She hadn't been well for a while, and something in Mary's voice confirmed my worst fears.

'Mam's been diagnosed with lung cancer.'

I felt the room spin. There's something in our family, a curse almost, when it comes to the lungs. Respiratory illnesses have haunted us for generations. The doctors said it was serious. Not much they could do. They offered some radiotherapy, maybe a few treatments to ease the pain, but there was no talk of a cure. Just borrowed time.

When I got that bombshell news, I was £3,000 behind on the mortgage for the house in Sandymount. That might not sound like much now, but back then, in 1989, it was a huge amount. And with everything falling apart and debts mounting up fast, I couldn't see a way out. Fear started creeping back in, the kind that sits on your chest at night and won't let you sleep. I couldn't bear the thought of my mother losing her home that she loved so much especially when she was so sick. It was her sanctuary.

And the thought that she might have to leave it? That she might not get to live out her final days in the comfort of her own home, surrounded by her own things, her familiar world? That would've broken me. I wouldn't have forgiven myself. I tried everything to get the money. I asked family, reached out to old contacts but £3,000 was a huge ask at the time, and no one had it to spare.

That house in Sandymount cost me nearly forty thousand, which was a huge amount back then. Not long ago I took a little trip down memory lane and drove past it. That same house sold recently for 1.5 million. That kind of thing makes you sick to your stomach. All I needed at the time to keep it was three thousand, but I just couldn't get it anywhere. Back then all I cared about was keeping it long enough so my mother could live out her final days in comfort.

She went downhill fast. Quicker than any of us expected. That made keeping the house in Sandymount essential. A place filled with comfort, with warmth, with memories. I couldn't imagine her final days spent anywhere else.

So, I kept pushing. I kept working, fighting tooth and nail to keep things afloat even though, deep down, I knew the house would have to go at some point. And when Mam's health worsened, my sisters Mary and Catherine all rallied around her. They were brilliant. They did what she had always done for us: they cared, they loved, they showed up. Mam had spent her whole life looking after everyone else. So now it was our turn.

Watching her fade away was the hardest part. A woman once so vibrant, so glamorous and strong. But little by little, we watched that strength drain away. She spent most of her time in bed, too weak to come downstairs. I would be there as often as I could, always dreading the moment I'd walk in and find her gone.

I'll never forget the day it happened in November 1989. The night before, I had seen her, kissed her on the forehead, tucked her in gently, and whispered 'I love you.' The next morning, I was over in Bachelor's Walk. I was clinging to hope, trying to secure a shop unit, for a furniture shop. I knew it was a long shot, but I had to try. I was desperate. Then the call came.

'Michael, you need to come now. Mam's taken a turn.'

I flew back to Sandymount in my little yellow Fiat, heart pounding, praying I'd make it in time. But I was thirty minutes late. She was gone – and I didn't get to say goodbye. The cruellest part of it? I've never been there at the end, not for any of them. Not once have I held the hand of a loved one in their final moments. It haunts me and some days, that weight feels unbearable.

When Mam passed away, it left a massive hole in our lives. She wasn't just our mother, she was the matriarch, the person we all turned to. Her presence was a constant comfort, and her absence was felt deeply and painfully. She was such a character, funny, wise, supportive, and she was always there for us. Her memory lives on in our stories, in the laughter we still share when we remember her quirks and her humour. And yes, in the sadness too.

The grief was overwhelming, but life doesn't stop. It was left to me as the eldest to organise her funeral. I went to Stafford's, arranged everything, and also took on the task of managing her estate. I tried to do everything properly, to honour her. But alongside the emotional toll, the financial strain weighed heavy on my shoulders and became suffocating.

Things started to unravel quickly. The banks were chasing me. I was falling behind on loan repayments, the direct debits weren't going through, and I couldn't pay my staff. Something had to give.

Managing both Mace shops along with the furniture businesses had proved to be too much. The Pearse Street store began to struggle, mainly due to theft. On top of that, I was too busy enjoying myself: living the high life, spending money and going out with women. I was young and careless. I thought I was Superman, that I could be everywhere at once. But I couldn't. The Mace shops weren't making any money. Overheads were piling up, and I couldn't keep up with the repayments. I was deep into my overdraft and it wasn't long before the bank came knocking. By then, I owed a lot. Much of the stock was bought on credit, and in layman's terms, I was screwed.

Eventually, I had to let go of the Mace shop on Pearse Street. I sold the lease to someone else. After that, the Ringsend shop also became too much to handle. I was in too much financial debt to keep it going, so I sold that lease as well. It became clear I needed to focus solely on the furniture business again. But even that wasn't enough to cover what I owed. I hated being in that position; I was deeply embarrassed about it. That's why I made the decision to sell the house in Sandymount to clear my debts. I managed to pay everyone off, but I ended up homeless. It was the Mace shops that caused the problems, and my own stupidity of course. I have no one to blame but myself.

I was left with only two things: the family shop on Pearse Street and the warehouse out in Coolock, which was packed with unsold furniture.

I had 14 employees and I had to let them all go. That was one of the hardest parts. I did my best to pay my suppliers back; some were understanding, others weren't. In the end, everything was gone. I tried everything, and I asked everyone I knew in the industry for help, but they turned their back on me.

Mary and I were homeless. I'll never forget that feeling of not having a home. I was so embarrassed and I would not wish that lost feeling on anyone. Mary ended up moving in with Catherine. It was a humbling, painful period. Once the house in Sandymount was gone, and I'd handed everything but Pearse Street back to the banks, I had a hundred quid to my name.

After all my hard work, the years of graft, lugging gas cylinders up and down stairs, selling everything I could, pushing myself day after day … I had almost nothing to show for it. I felt completely disillusioned.

I met up with Mary and we spent the last of my money on a lovely afternoon. We drank in the pub, we laughed and we cried. I think it was exactly what we needed. It was cathartic. At that point, it felt like nothing else could go wrong, everything that could go wrong already had. So why not?

We were in a 'fuck it' kind of mood, and honestly, it was very much needed. Mary was more than happy to be my drinking partner, because at that stage, though I didn't know it, she had a problem with the booze.

But in the middle of that hardship, something beautiful happened. Margaret and I started to grow closer. Our bond deepened, mainly because of the shared love for our daughter, Michelle. We both knew she needed stability. She needed a real home, something solid to grow up in. Somehow, I pulled together enough to rent a small house in Clontarf. Margaret and I moved in together, and something shifted, we started building a life. And over time our love strengthened. It was then I started to embrace fatherhood and understood what it meant to have someone depend on you for everything.

When Michelle was much younger, she would constantly ask me for a treehouse. At the time, we didn't have the money to do it, and I really wanted her to have one. So instead, I told her a story.

I said that when I was a child, I had lived in a magical forest, and there was a man there who grew trees of all sorts. He was growing special trees to provide the wood for her treehouse. That's why it was taking so long, the trees needed time to grow. I promised her that once this man had finished growing the trees, he would send the wood, and I would build her treehouse. It was just going to take a little while. She bought it, hook, line and sinker.

Whenever our friends came over, Michelle would proudly tell them all about this magical tree forest. I'd join in, adding how I used to get chased by lions, tigers and bears when I lived in this fantastic place as a child. The kids would listen wide-eyed, completely believing every word.

I'll never forget the day I finally got enough money together to get the treehouse and have it all set up in the garden for when she came home from school. Michelle came home and saw the treehouse in the garden. Her face lit up in amazement. I told her, 'The forest man finally grew all the trees and sent the wood over to Ireland.' She was overjoyed and ran straight to the treehouse, shouting for joy every step of the way.

Michelle and I used to dance around the dining room together. It reminded me of my own childhood days, of my father dancing with me and my sisters around the kitchen. Sometimes, we would even climb onto the dining table and dance around like lunatics, laughing and spinning. Michelle and I were growing closer and I was learning how to become a dad. I wanted to create happy memories with her old man for her to look back on.

I also used to take Michelle and her friends in my work van to Clara Lara, the fun park in Wicklow. There were usually about five of them, all desperate to go. So I got an old sofa, secured it in the back of the van, and off we went. Of course, you wouldn't be able to do that sort of thing today. They sat back there laughing, screaming and singing all the way down. They had an absolute whale of a time. These were some of the best memories we made as father and daughter, and I think Michelle realised early on that her father was a bit of a lunatic.

In later years, when Michelle went through her first heartbreak after breaking up with her first boyfriend at 20, I was able to be there for her completely. There's nothing that breaks a father's heart more than seeing his daughter's heart broken.

I gently encouraged her to do a novena. Now, we're not exactly 'holy Joes', not by a long stretch, but I've always found comfort in doing a novena when I've faced troubles in my own life. A novena is a nine-day prayer, where each day you offer a specific prayer or set of prayers with a particular intention.

My go-to saint has always been St Jude, the patron saint of hopeless situations and desperate cases. Michelle and I started going to church together once a week, praying to St Jude over the course of ten weeks. What began as a spiritual act became a beautiful bonding time for us. After each visit, we'd go out for something to eat and talk about how she was getting on.

Week by week, I saw the light slowly return to her. By the final novena, she was doing much better, and we had all but forgotten he-who-shall-not-be-named. I've always believed that things happen for a reason. If that break-up hadn't happened, she might never have met her husband, and they wouldn't have their beautiful children today.

Back in the late eighties and early nineties, I felt like I had failed in so many ways; at least I was beginning to succeed as a father and I was not giving up without a fight. I held onto something. I refused to give up on myself. Maybe it was because I'd seen my parents survive so many tough times. They never gave in. They just kept going, even when things were at their worst. That's what I had to do. Keep going.

One blessing was the deal my family had with the shop on Pearse Street: it was €150 a year for rent, with an 86-year lease. I worked it as hard as I could. I sold everything I could get my hands on. If it wasn't nailed down, I was selling it. I reached out for favours. Friends who were suppliers gave me stock. Some of them saved me, and I am forever grateful to them for that. I kept pushing, I had no choice. I was going to white-knuckle this time and get through it somehow. I had a daughter to think about. I wasn't going to fold and give in.

Eventually, after begging and borrowing from everyone and everywhere, I found my footing again. I could just about provide for my wife and child. I started to save a little money. Against all the odds, I managed to secure a lease for a furniture shop in the Northside Shopping Centre. Someone was looking down on me for sure. I registered the company as *Northside Furniture Limited,* and it did well.

It was a good shop with great staff, and I ran it for 26 years, but I have one very bad memory connected to it. One night in 1993, when Michelle was about seven, I was coming home from that shop. At the time, we were still living in a rented house in Clontarf. In those days, you brought the day's takings home with you, so I had a briefcase full of money.

As I was about to open the front door, I suddenly felt a presence behind me. I turned around, and there stood a well-built man wearing a balaclava. I froze in fear. When I looked down, I saw a large knife in his hand. He stepped closer and pressed the knife against my stomach. Then he reached for the briefcase and tried to yank it from my hands.

But something in me just wouldn't let go. I needed that money desperately, and I thought, I'm not handing it over, I'll never get it back. He kept pulling at the case, but being the stubborn man I can be, I wasn't letting go. The struggle went on for a few tense moments.

Caroline, Margaret's sister, was in the house and saw what was happening through the window. She shouted, 'Michael, let go of the case, for God's sake!' But I wasn't having any of it. Nothing was going to make me let go of my hard-earned cash.

Then Caroline came out, and can you believe it, she kicked me in the leg! This traumatic event was starting to turn into an almost comical farce. As she kicked me, the suitcase went flying out of my hands. The mugger grabbed it and took off running. I ran after him, and Caroline ran after me, yelling, 'Michael, just leave it!'

Someone trying to rob you on your own doorstep is probably one of the most invasive things that can happen. I never caught him, and I never got the money back. But to this day, I still have my suspicions about who it might have been.

Not long after I opened the shop in the Northside Shopping Centre, I launched a bedroom furniture store in the Donaghmede Shopping Centre, then one in Capel Street and another on Aughrim Street. Slowly but surely, I started rebuilding not just the business, but my sense of self-worth. There was hope again, for me, for my family, for our future.

At the time Margaret and I didn't want to rent any more as it was just money down the drain and we were really hoping to get enough together to get a mortgage. One day she called me from Clontarf. She'd just walked past a house on Kincora Road and it was for sale. She was excited, and I could hear the joy in her voice. We went to see it together, and it felt perfect. We both saw it as our forever home. I met with the bank, managed to get the mortgage, and we were over the moon. We had our home, the businesses were steady, and we had our beautiful daughter. Things were finally on an even keel.

Chapter 11

From Russia with Love

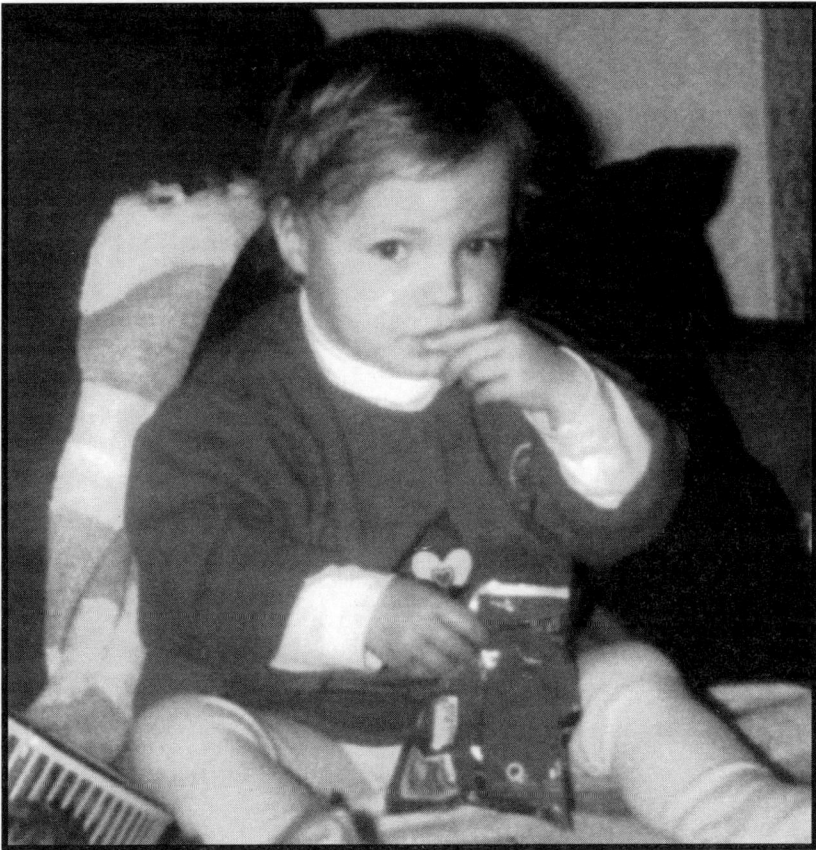

Margaret yearned for more children. She loved being a mother, but we struggled to conceive again. We weren't sure why, whether it was me or her, but it just wasn't happening.

Until it did. The second time Margaret became pregnant, we were over the moon. I remember the day so clearly, the way she burst through the door after coming back from the doctor's. Her face was lit up like I'd never seen before, tears of joy in her eyes as she told me the news. She was hysterically happy. Becoming a mother again was something she longed for with all her heart, and in that moment, it felt like life had finally given her the blessing she'd been waiting for.

She threw herself into every little detail, imagining names, and talking to Michelle about becoming a big sister. There was a lightness in her. I think they call that the glow of a pregnant woman. Sadly, a few weeks later, everything changed.

I came home from work one evening, tired as usual, but as soon as I stepped into the house I knew something was wrong. The silence was heavy. I found Margaret curled up on the sofa in the front room, her face pale, eyes swollen and red. I rushed to her and asked what had happened.

She could barely get the words out, but she didn't need to, I already knew. 'I lost the baby,' she whispered. And then she just broke down, folding in on herself like the pain was too much to carry. I sat beside her, trying to comfort her, but felt utterly helpless. There are no words in moments like that, only silence and presence. I held her as tightly as I could, wishing I could take the pain away, knowing I couldn't.

It was one of the most heartbreaking moments of our lives. The joy we had felt just weeks before had been replaced by a devastating emptiness and all I could do was sit there and grieve with her.

Margaret was a strong woman, stronger than most people ever realised and she carried on with life, as so many women do when faced with a pain like that. In time, we decided to try again. Ten months later, she was pregnant and we were of course over the moon.

I could see the hope in her eyes, but also the fear. Margaret was cautious this time. She didn't tell many people, almost as if saying it out loud might make it happen again. She carried for three months this time, and then, once again, it wasn't meant to be.

Her heart was broken. She started to believe something was wrong with her, like her body had somehow failed her. I tried everything I could to reassure her, to remind her that none of this was her fault, that these things just happen, sometimes without reason. But I don't think my words ever reached the part of her that was truly hurting.

After the second miscarriage, we sat down together and made the decision to try one more time. We didn't say it out loud, but we both knew it would be the last. Whatever was happening, it was beyond our control. And when the third pregnancy ended the same way, I knew without her even needing to say a word that Margaret couldn't go through it again.

We looked in another direction and came across the Chernobyl Children's Project, an organisation founded by Adi Roche in 1991 that brought children from the Chernobyl region to Ireland, mainly so they could breathe clean air and experience a safer, more peaceful environment. Margaret and I were deeply moved by the children affected by the Chernobyl disaster.

We took part in the project for several years, welcoming children into our home during the summer months. They'd stay with us for two or three months at a time, and they absolutely loved being in Ireland. We made a real effort to give them a special experience, we showed them around Dublin, and to them it felt like stepping into a fairytale compared to what they had come from. There was a wonderful community of families here in Ireland also hosting children, and we became close with many of them.

Margaret especially loved having the children in our home. They were such lovely kids, so polite, so grateful. I think they were amazed by Ireland and what it felt like to breathe in the fresh, crisp air. Margaret would often get teary when it was time for them to leave. She grew so attached to them and hated saying goodbye. We continued with the project for several years, and it was something we truly cherished. It gave us a deep sense of purpose, knowing that, in some small way, we were helping these children escape, even briefly, from the tragedy that had turned their world upside down.

Eventually, we decided we wanted to adopt. But we hit a wall in Ireland: I was considered too old. On a side note, I think the age rules around adoption are ridiculous in this country. There are so many loving, stable people in their 40s and 50s who would make incredible parents, but they're denied the chance while children are stuck in an uncaring system when they could have the chance of a loving home. I find that insane. It's something that really needs to change.

After a lot of research and many conversations, we decided to adopt from Russia. An agency guided us through every step of the process. We were only the second couple in Ireland to adopt from Russia and we got to know the first couple very well.

We underwent two years of assessment by the Eastern Health Board. It was invasive. Every question you could imagine, we had to answer: Why adopt? Why not have your own children? How often do you have sex? Nothing was off limits.

One requirement we couldn't get around: we had to be married. So Margaret and I made the decision. It wasn't a romantic proposal, it was practical. We knew it was what we needed to do. We had a tiny wedding in Killiney in October 1995 with just five guests. It was intimate but a meaningful ceremony. My best man was Frankie O'Rourke, his partner Martina was there, my two sisters, Mary and Catherine, and Margaret's mother. That was it. A simple ceremony, a small reception in a local hotel. It was a lovely day.

I never imagined that after all those years of looking out at the scrapyard from the back of Pearse Street, the family who owned it would one day become my in-laws. Maybe it's true, after searching for love everywhere else, sometimes the right person is waiting in your own backyard.

Now we were married we could move ahead with the adoption process. The agency sent us photographs of several children and we were asked to choose the one we'd like to adopt. Margaret had her heart set on a little girl from the very beginning. I think if I had given her the go-ahead, she would've taken them all, that's just who she was. Every single child tugged at her heartstrings, but then she saw her, the sweetest little girl with the gentlest eyes. Her name was Marina and she was two years old.

The moment Margaret laid eyes on her, she knew. There was no hesitation, no second guessing. That was our daughter. And so, we asked to adopt Marina. As soon as the paperwork was approved, we flew to Russia.

The journey to Russia was a night none of us will forget. It was the same night Princess Diana died – 31 August 1997. Margaret was devastated. She loved Princess Diana, and the flight to Russia was one of joy mixed with sorrow.

Once we landed in Russia, we took an overnight train from Moscow to reach Marina's orphanage in Nizhny Novgorod. The hotel we were put in was awfully dark, cold and depressing. It reminded me of Ireland in the 1950s.

Before we were even allowed to set foot in the orphanage, we had to appear in court and what we experienced there was nothing short of bizarre. The questions we were asked were outrageous, even disturbing. And they didn't spare Michelle, either.

At the time, there was a horrible rumour circulating that some American families were adopting Russian children just to harvest their organs. As in, taking children's body parts to save their own. I still can't wrap my head around it. It's absolutely disgusting, and the fact that such a thing even needed to be considered fills me with rage and disbelief. Sometimes I just don't understand the world. I don't understand people.

Because of those suspicions, every foreign family adopting a Russian child had to go through the courts. We had to stand in front of a judge, like we were on trial. The process was intense, uncomfortable and deeply personal. We were asked question after question, some of them understandable, others just bizarre.

'Do you have any other children?'

'Are any of them sick?'

'Do they suffer from anything?'

I answered every question through the interpreter, as did Margaret and Michelle. And it didn't stop there. They wanted to know everything:

'Why do you want to adopt?'

'Why did you come to Russia?'

'Why this child?'

It wasn't a quick formality; it was two full hours in court. Two hours of being examined, judged and, in many ways, doubted. The tone was serious, even accusatory. You could feel the weight of suspicion in the room.

And then, this part still gets me, they brought Michelle, our daughter, into a separate room. They questioned her too. They asked her directly, 'Are you sick?' Just to make sure we weren't lying.

Now, part of me understands the reasoning behind it. Maybe it's good they were thorough. Maybe it's right that they were trying to protect these vulnerable children. But the way it was done, the coldness, the suspicion, it was painful. It was humiliating. And it was heartbreaking to see Michelle subjected to that. We were there to give a child a home, a family and love. And yet we were treated like criminals under investigation.

After we finished in the court and all was finally approved, we made our way to the orphanage the next morning. It was shabby, run-down, overcrowded, overrun with feral cats, and there was a sickening stench. It was definitely not the kind of place that should be home to children. On our way to Marina, we passed through a corridor or common area where many of the other children were gathered. As we walked by, they began shouting out 'Mama! Papa! Mama! Papa!' in Russian. It was overwhelming. Gut-wrenching. So many children, all hoping that maybe this time, someone had come for them. Margaret would have swooped them all up in her arms and taken them back with her if she could have.

Eventually, we were introduced to the manager of the orphanage. We had an interpreter with us, a lovely young woman named Farida. She was warm and empathetic, and she helped us understand Marina's story.

We didn't spend much time there; our focus was meeting Marina and bringing her home. The first time we saw her, she was sitting at a table all by herself, quietly eating her dinner. There was no one tending to her, no one offering comfort or company. Just this little girl in a big, grey room, silently eating on her own.

She had a big blue bow in her hair, and she looked so lovely, truly beautiful. The image of her sitting there alone was so sad. We were struck by it. We sat down around the table with her, trying to bring some warmth into that cold room. Margaret gently went over and fed her, spooning food into her mouth with care. It was such a tender moment.

In the middle of that bleak institution was this tiny girl who stole our hearts the moment we laid eyes on her. Michelle was with us too, and it was as if Marina just instantly belonged. She felt like family right from the start.

We were told that Marina had been abandoned, left on the steps of the orphanage. There were no records of her family, no trace of siblings, though we were told her mother had other children. By all accounts, Marina's mother was a married woman who had an affair with a soldier, which resulted in Marina's birth.

Her mother's name was Olga, and the father's name was Albert. Well, that's what we had been told. From what we could gather, Olga was a woman who had lived a somewhat wild life. She had made her choices, perhaps sought love in the wrong places.

And there, in the middle of it all, was Marina, this beautiful little gift to the world who was now to become our daughter. From the very beginning, she felt like she was already ours and this was meant to be.

Marina was so tiny, and she had absolutely no idea what was happening. It was no surprise that she was understandably distressed on the flight home. She was terrified, crying loudly, confused and overwhelmed by the noise, the strange faces and the sudden change in her world.

As the flight went on, other passengers started to realise what was happening. Word spread that we had just adopted a child from Russia, and it became a topic of conversation on board. At the time, we were only the second couple in Ireland to adopt from Russia, so it was a big deal, a real talking point. People were curious, supportive and, thankfully, very kind.

The air hostesses were especially lovely. They were incredibly attentive, helping us with anything we needed. Marina, despite her tears, quickly became the star of the plane. People were fascinated by her, and many came over to wish us well.

Eventually, Margaret managed to calm Marina down, gently rocking her until she finally fell asleep in her arms. Every time I think back to that moment, I still get emotional.

We landed in Shannon Airport, where I had left the car, and we drove back to Dublin. We arrived home in the afternoon, exhausted but thankful. What we hadn't expected was the attention waiting for us.

As we pulled up to the house, we were met with a crowd. People were gathered outside, neighbours, well-wishers and even news reporters, all wanting to know more about the adoption and about Marina. I was stunned. It was far bigger than I ever imagined. Even American newspapers reached out for interviews. The whole thing had taken on a life of its own.

As soon as Marina stepped out of the car outside our house in Clontarf, she ran straight into the arms of Margaret's step-mother, as if they had known each other forever. They embraced so naturally, without hesitation. Chrissie was such a warm, welcoming woman, and Marina must have sensed that immediately. Her instant connection with Chrissie helped Marina feel a little more at home in those very first few minutes.

Not long after the adoption, we were invited onto the radio, and Pat Kenny had me on his show to talk about our experience. Following that, Brendan and Inga Maloney, who ran the agency we had used, asked if we would consider helping others. They wanted to bring the organisation to more people and thought we could play a role in supporting families hoping to adopt from Russia.

We agreed without hesitation. Margaret and I knew how overwhelming the process could be, and we were more than happy to help. People began coming to our home with questions, sometimes just looking for guidance, sometimes needing reassurance. We did whatever we could to support them.

It was a whirlwind time. One of the newspapers even ran a full article on us, featuring a photo of me, Margaret and Marina. The headline read: 'From Russia with Love'.

Looking back now, it all feels like a dream: emotional, chaotic and deeply meaningful. Also, it made me realise the power that the media have and how it can get stories out to so many so quickly.

It felt like something out of a fairy tale. I suppose, in some way, I became her Daddy Warbucks, which she often calls me when she's tapping me for money. Marina came home with us and became our daughter, our family. Michelle adored her new little sister, and the love in our home doubled overnight.

Margaret was so happy and fulfilled. The shops were doing well, business was steady, and for the first time in a long while, life felt whole again. I was a proud father, a husband, a provider. We had survived the dark times, and we had come through stronger, more united as a family.

Marina was a beautiful little girl and full of personality. From the very first moment we met her, it felt as though she had always been a part of our family. There was no adjustment period, no awkwardness. She simply belonged with us, as naturally and easily as if she had been there from the beginning. It's hard to put into words just how quickly and deeply she nestled into all our hearts.

She had a natural friendliness and everyone adored her. Very affectionate, she was always ready with a hug, holding our hands and wanting cuddles on the couch. Marina was wonderfully tactile in that way.

The truth is we fell head over heels for her, every single one of us. And you could see that she loved us just as much in return, she would run across the room into your arms without a second thought. Which was a huge relief considering how difficult her start was. At that stage in our lives, we were in a place where we could afford to give her little extras, the sweets, the toys, the days out. Margaret was so grateful to have another child to love and take care of.

Looking back now, it's hard to even imagine what life would have been like without her. It feels almost impossible, as if there's a version of our lives without Marina that simply couldn't have existed. She didn't just fit into our family; she became an essential part of it.

Chapter 12

The Good Times

It was the mid-1990s and things were flying. I mean, the money was rolling in like waves at Dollymount, and the banks? Well, they were practically begging you to take it. You could've walked in with a balaclava on your head and walked out with a mortgage. It was madness, beautiful, glittering madness. And I was right in the thick of it, loving every second.

My company, Northside Furniture Limited, was flying too. Business was booming so much I decided to open a second shop in Finglas Shopping Centre. The Pearse Street shop was out the door, the warehouse in Coolock was moving serious stock.

I was living in Clontarf and driving to Coolock every day. I thought, 'How can I make this journey earn me a few quid?' So, I got my PSV license and bought a blue Skoda Octavia taxi. I still have it today. People sometimes flag me down thinking I'm working and I'll give them a lift, no charge. I just love meeting people and having chats with people. It's great fun especially if they recognise me. They roar, 'You're Mattress Mick!' It makes their day, the fact that Mattress Mick has taken them to where they need to go. I think some of them think someone has slipped something in their drink they are that shocked. For me, though, that's part of the fun, doing mad outlandish things that people don't forget.

The taxi business was getting busier and a friend of mine said he was trying to rent a taxi. So I rented him mine for a while. That few hundred quid a week helped me buy another car. Then another. This was not planned, but before long, I had 28 taxis on the road. But that's me – I never do things by half. That business kept me going during tough times. It was completely separate from the furniture business and never part of any liquidation.

If you needed something, anything, from furniture to a cab or a contact, I was your man. People used to joke that I had a guy for everything, and half the time, that guy was me. The girls were doing well, everyone was looked after, and, truth be told, I'd started enjoying myself a bit more too. Fancy motors, nights out, the odd holiday, a second house to rent out, life was good. The Celtic Tiger wasn't just purring, it was roaring, and we were all roaring right along with it.

My mates were buying properties left, right and centre, flipping them, doing them up, selling them again. You'd swear we were all real estate moguls the way we were carrying on. And sure, we thought it would never end. This was our time. After generations of struggle and misery, Ireland was finally cashing in, and we were waving our green flags and green money like there was no tomorrow.

It felt like Ireland had suddenly switched into full technicolour. After decades of emigration, hardship and modest living, the country seemed to explode with money, opportunity and a fair few notions too.

You could feel the change everywhere, like a pulse running through the country. Dublin was absolutely teeming with new business. Construction cranes pierced the skyline, and new hotels, apartment blocks and shopping centres seemed to spring up overnight. Everything was being built, everyone had work and plenty of it.

What was truly heart-warming was seeing people coming home. People who had emigrated to America or Australia were returning, bringing their families with them. Airports were filled with hugs and happy tears. Families reunited after years apart. There was work to come home to and for once, a future here.

Ireland had developed a bit of a swagger, and with it came a real sense of confidence. It felt like the good times would never end. The money was flowing, and we were having the time of our lives. Credit was easy, businesses were booming and the pubs were absolutely heaving. Even the music on the radio sounded cheerier. You'd see people in the city eating sushi, and trendy cafés popping up on every corner. We had become the land of cappuccinos and frothy mochas. Brown Thomas bags swinging from arms like status symbols.

And we were dreaming bigger than ever before. Suddenly, being Irish was cool. After years of being underestimated and being the butt of the joke, we were the ones flying high. Irish boy bands were topping the charts and there was a global fascination with our culture. If you were Irish, your name was on the mat and there was a welcome there for you. That alone marked a massive shift from how things used to be.

House prices were skyrocketing. Everything seemed possible. It was mad. But for once, we had a taste of the good life and we devoured it. Ordinary people were suddenly driving BMWs or cruising around in big Land Rovers. Friends of mine were buying second homes abroad, planning long-haul holidays and living large in ways we'd never imagined before.

I wasn't any different from anyone else, to be honest. As soon as the chance arose, I was off to Spain like a shot. I loved it. The sun, the beaches, the cheap food and wine, we were, as the young would say nowadays, living our best life. It was always me and the lads heading off: Noel, Harry and Brian.

Every year without fail, we went to Puerto Banús. We booked the same apartment by the sea and off we went to Spain with flip-flops and dreams. You'd have sworn we were a bunch of 20-somethings the way we carried on, except the only six-packs we were carrying were under our arms and not under our T-shirts. We were old enough to know better, but absolutely young enough inside to still do it all anyway.

The plan was always simple: book flights, pack, hire a car and pretend to be millionaires for a week. We'd land, pick up a little motor and set off exploring. Frank Sinatra would be blaring out the windows like we were in Vegas instead of some dusty Spanish backroad dodging potholes the size of swimming pools. Those were the days. We lived it up. Drinking started early, hair of the dog to cure the dog that bit you the night before. We'd be having the craic from morning till night, meeting all the locals, charming the ladies, eating our own body weight in tapas, and drinking sangria on the beach.

The wine was €1.50 for a bottle at the time, which was either great or dangerous. The food was even better, a few quid for a massive plate of fresh seafood – much cheaper than booming Ireland. Everything was just easy, no worries, no responsibilities, just pure craic with the lads like the rest of the Irish were doing at the time.

One night, Noel, Harry, Brian and I were having a little jaunt around the Puerto Banús pubs. And as you can imagine, after a few bottles of cheap wine and a good few beers our decision-making was ... let's say, questionable.

We stumbled across this little club tucked down a side street. Now, if any of us had been fully sober, we might have taken more notice of the red neon signs flashing like a dodgy Christmas tree, or the way the bouncer was eyeing us up and down in a threatening manner. But we were four innocent Catholic boys, born and bred, so of course we just wandered right in without a second thought.

Inside, it was dark and smoky, and it pulsed with upbeat music. We parked ourselves at a table, ordered a round of drinks, and looked around.

Now, it didn't take long to notice that the 'customers' were few and far between, and most of the people inside were, how do I put this, very friendly women wearing very little clothing. But did we click immediately? No. We just thought, 'God, the people here are so outgoing! What a lovely town!'

We were chatting away, having a good time, when this stunning woman came over to me. She was tall with long, dark hair and olive skin. She was absolutely beautiful and the lads were a little puzzled. Naturally, I was thinking, *Well, well, well. Looks like old Mick's still got it.* She was a nice lady and we chatted for a bit, but the lads didn't know what to make of it. Maybe I had turned into the George Clooney of Puerto Banús and no one had told me.

After a bit more laughing and outrageous flirting with me, she leaned in close, real close, and whispered something in my ear. She told me, very politely, the price list for her services. I couldn't believe what I was hearing. That is the first time I'd ever been propositioned like that. I nearly launched myself off the stool in shock. I looked at Noel, Harry and Brian with the horror of a man who's just realised where he was.

'We're in a brothel!' I practically shouted. The lads collapsed in hysterics. I said to the lady 'Thank you very much for your extremely kind offer, but I think we'll be moving on. I hope you enjoy the rest of your evening.' And off we staggered, laughing, into the night to find somewhere we could safely have a pint without accidentally getting more than we bargained for.

Those were the days, my friends. The good times in Spain. I still go over to Marbella to visit but it's much more low-key these days. I stay with my good friend, Dennis Carroll, who lives there. There's a big Irish community and a lot of them recognise me, even in Spain. Jackie McNulty, another friend of mine, owns a bar called McNulty's in Marbella. She has cardboard cut-outs of me in the pub and dresses me up as Father Christmas.

The good times were not just good, they were fantastic. But, as always with every high, comes the crash. Fast-forward to 2008. No one was expecting this reversal of fortunes: the shit hit the fan and didn't miss Ireland.

With the collapse of Lehman Brothers, the stock markets tumbled. It was the biggest financial crash the world had seen for decades. The carnage spread across the financial sector globally. Ireland's Celtic Tiger had uttered its terminal breath and the party was officially over.

The panic across the country was profound and everyone held on as tight as they could, waiting for it to be quickly fixed by those in power. But it was too late, the damage had been done. The Tiger did a runner, tail between its legs. It disappeared back into the jungle, leaving devastation behind. One minute we were on top of the world, and the next, boom, everything collapsed. The economy tanked, and with it, my businesses, my plans and my dreams.

That newfound confidence quickly gave way to anger and shame. Our optimism vanished. Shops were shutting down left, right and centre. House prices plummeted, leaving many people in negative equity, owing more on their mortgages than their homes were worth. Countless families couldn't keep up with repayments, and repossessions began. Construction ground to a halt overnight.

Jobs disappeared. Unemployment soared. New graduates couldn't find work. Everything had fallen apart. And just like that, we became a nation of emigration once again, our young people packing their bags for Australia, the UK and the US. Families were torn apart. The banks had taken enormous risks; bailing them out cost us over €64 billion.

Everything was affected: public services, tax rates and pension cuts. Throughout Ireland, a deep sense of betrayal rippled through every part of life. Schools suffered, healthcare services were strained and the welfare system took a hit. Ordinary people were left paying for the recklessness of bankers and developers.

Our trust in the government and politicians quickly crumbled. It was a brutal wake-up call, not just about how the banks operated, but how the government failed us too. We were the ones left to foot the bill.

Many of my friends in retail were struggling, just like I was again. People were panicking, rents shot through the roof, nobody was spending and I was left holding the bag. I had no choice but to close the shops in Capel Street, Aughrim Street and Donaghmede Shopping Centre. I couldn't pay the staff. Suppliers were knocking. Debts piled up once more. I hated having to close them down and let people go, but I had no choice. It was a mess.

I thought if I could just save the shop in the Northside Shopping Centre we would be all right. All the reserves and profits I had built up over the years were being poured back into Northside Furniture Limited, to try and save it because I truly believed I could turn it around, but by then it was too late. The landlords still demanded their rent, which was going up, the service charges were astronomical, and sales kept dropping drastically.

Eventually, I made the decision to liquidate Northside Furniture Limited. I went through the full, proper liquidation process and it was one of the hardest things I've ever had to do. I had to gather everyone I owed money to in a hotel room, look them in the eye and apologise profusely. It was a horrible experience. In those circumstances, you feel incredibly alone, like there's no way out. Above all, you feel judged, looked down upon. If there was something else I could have done, I would have, but I had exhausted every avenue. Facing the people I owed money to was incredibly tough. The process of going through everything went on for hours. It was like someone picking up all the bad decisions you ever made and rubbing them in your face.

I settled what I could with my suppliers. Most of them were decent – they knew I wasn't out to shaft anyone. Some were understanding and others didn't want to know. I returned what stock I could from the shops. Because of the long-standing lease I had on the Pearse Street shop and the Coolock warehouse I was able to hold on to them. But I was wiped. Shattered. And again, starting from scratch. I had no money, no stock and no staff.

I just about managed to save the house. I remember thinking, *how the hell did I let this happen? Again?* We were all hypnotised by the Tiger, and when it bit us on the arse, we didn't even see it coming. The whole thing was a disaster and I had no idea what to do.

Now, looking back, it was also the best thing that ever happened to me. Out of the ashes of Northside Furniture Limited came something new, something better, even though at the time I couldn't see it. When you're down like that it's hard to see past it, hard to look ahead, but I had a family and no choice.

The only thing ticking along were the taxis. They just about kept the lights on. Around this time in 2008, I had a call in to do a taxi run from Dublin Airport all the way up to Belfast. It wasn't a regular request – not exactly a short spin across town – but I needed the money. So I took the job. I quoted the fare at €150 for the trip. Considering it was a good two-hour drive, I thought that was fair, and they agreed.

When I pulled up at the airport, I spotted them easily: a cheerful-looking couple standing near the arrivals hall with their cases, still on a holiday high. They were full of smiles, full of stories about their trip. It turned out they'd just come back from Tenerife. The man said he was an accountant for one of the big supermarket chains. He seemed like a solid, professional type; his partner worked at a school and they seemed like a genuinely nice couple.

We set off, and the conversation flowed easily. They told me about their holiday and how much they enjoyed it. I shared a few of my own travel stories too, and before we knew it, the miles were slipping away.

Eventually, we rolled into Belfast, weaving through the suburbs until we reached a big housing estate where they lived. I pulled up outside their place, hopped out of the car and started unloading their luggage from the boot, still chatting away like we were old pals. Then, without warning they grabbed their bags and bolted. Just like that.

For a few seconds, I just stood there in complete shock, absolutely gobsmacked. It took a moment to register what had just happened. They hadn't paid me. They just took off into the estate, disappearing between the houses, leaving me standing there in the middle of God-knows-where in Belfast.

As I sat back down in the car and turned the key, another harsh reality hit me: the petrol light was flashing. I barely had enough fuel left in the tank to make it across town, never mind the two-hour drive back to Dublin. I'd been counting on that money. I needed it not just to earn it but to pay for the fuel to get home.

I sat there for a minute, wondering what to do. I was half-thinking I imagined it and they had just nipped into their house and they would run back out with the money at any second. They didn't. I was stuck far from home, no safety net, no one to turn to and no money.

I decided to drive with the petrol I had left to the nearest petrol station, praying the fumes in the tank would carry me there. When I pulled in, I explained the whole situation to a man behind the counter. I must've looked half desperate because he didn't hesitate. He just nodded, smiled and said, 'Sure, we'll sort you out.'

He filled the tank for me, trusting me on nothing more than my word that I'd send the money back once I got home. Just simple kindness from one human being to another. I was so grateful. After what had just happened with that couple, my faith in people had taken a knock. And yet here was a stranger showing me that decency was still alive and well in the world.

Thankfully, I made it home safely. That was the only time anything like that ever happened to me. Most of the people I picked up over the years were good, generous with tips and respectful enough not to run off.

After winding down Northside Furniture Limited, I started another business, *Beds Plus*. It wasn't a limited company, just a name to keep trading under. I sold the small amount of stock I could get hold of, thanks to a few understanding suppliers but I was scraping by, literally week by week. It was touch and go constantly. Loans from friends, favours here and there. Every month was a balancing act. I lived in a state of permanent anxiety, waking up each day unsure how I'd get through the next.

That's when I started to see my father in myself. I remembered how he worried when things went wrong, the toll it took on him. His health. His spirit. Sometimes, I think it was the worry that brought him to an early grave and I didn't want that. Not for me. Not for my family.

Chapter 13

The Birth of Mattress Mick

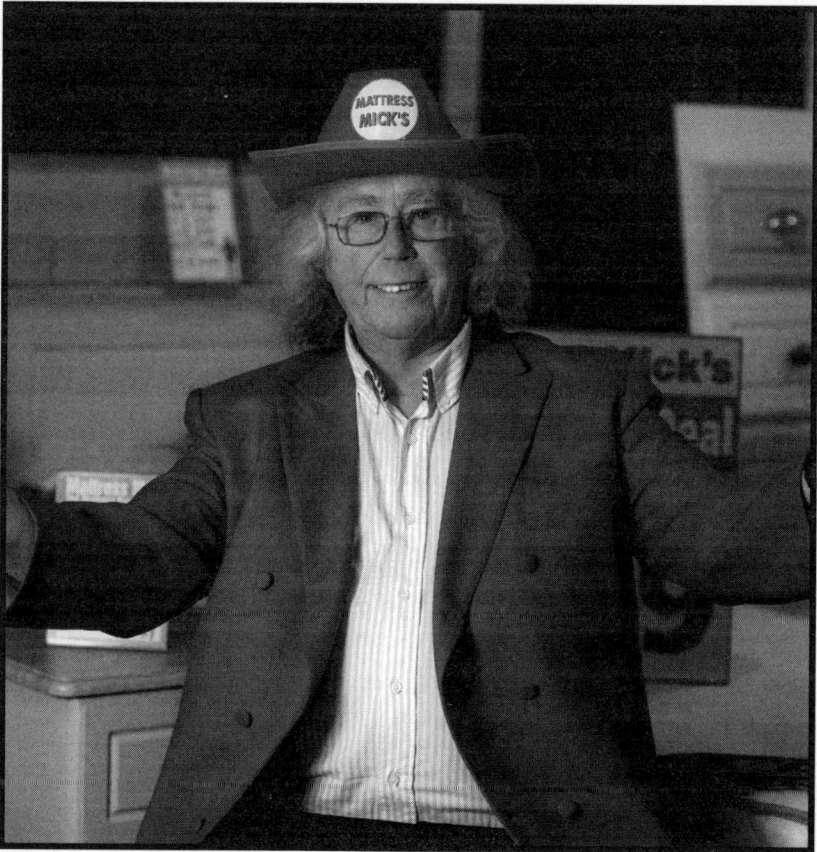

Chapter 13

The Birth of Mattress Mick

Luckily I had sold the warehouse stock and

So that was where I was that fateful evening in The Yacht, when I ran into Paul Kelly. Within a few days, we'd had our second meeting in the same pub, and Mattress Mick was born. Our slogan was: 'Irish-made mattresses at unbelievable prices.' Genius.

Paul threw himself into helping me build the Mattress Mick persona. He set up the social media pages, started filming videos, and before I knew it, things started moving fast. We took a photo outside the shop on Pearse Street, me with a big cheesy grin and my hand stuck out like I was mid-high-five. That picture blew up online. It became *the* image. The unofficial Mattress Mick logo. The red jacket I wear would also become synonymous as my Mattress Mick costume.

We went full guerrilla warfare on the marketing front, with posters, flyers, even cardboard cut-outs of my mug. You couldn't walk down the street without bumping into me. Luckily, I had a few mates who helped me with stock, and the momentum was building. Mattress Mick, the mattress price fighter was suddenly everywhere.

Things had already started picking up, and Mattress Mick was making small waves but nothing could have prepared me for this. One day in 2015, completely out of the blue, we found out that Stephen Fry – yes, the Stephen Fry, the English national treasure – had spotted the posters of me up by the

Five Lamps. There I was with a big cheesy grin, arms flung out. It's no surprise he saw me: like the rest of Dublin, he had no choice.

But not only did he see me, he tweeted about it. He shared a photo of one of my posters with a caption that said, 'One day I hope to meet "Mattress Mick". I think we'll have lots to discuss. Mattresses for example. And price.' I nearly dropped the phone when I saw it.

The internet exploded. The tweet went absolutely mental. I'm talking tens of thousands of likes and retweets. People were tagging their mates, sharing it in group chats, quoting it with things like 'only in Ireland' and 'the hero we didn't know we needed'. That gave me a real kick of confidence. I began to see a light at the end of a long, arduous tunnel. Could Mattress Mick be the answer? Was this finally the moment in my life when everything would fall into place?

Suddenly, everyone was talking about Mattress Mick. People who had never heard of me before were now googling me, messaging me, following my socials. And the best part? *Stephen bloody Fry* knew who I was. He was only in Dublin for a few days, I think. Maybe shooting something, I'm not sure. Whatever the reason, he saw me. And just like that, I went from a local madman with a mattress business to a national cult hero.

Paul saw an opportunity the moment it happened. You've never seen a man spring into action so fast. He was determined to somehow get Stephen Fry into the shop. 'Imagine the photo,' he said. 'You and Stephen Fry, shaking hands next to a stack of mattresses.' I thought he was mad. 'Paul,' I told him, 'Stephen Fry's not coming in here, he's not going to wander down to Pearse Street for a selfie with me in front of the memory foam section.'

But Paul was undeterred. Nothing ventured, nothing gained, right? He even offered Stephen Fry a free mattress and said he could take his pick of anything in the shop if he popped in for a quick photo. I laughed and said, 'Where's he going to put it? In the overhead locker on his Ryanair flight?' Still, the offer was made.

Stephen Fry was gone with the Dublin breeze. We did get a 'thanks but it's not possible on this occasion email', but did we sulk? Not a chance. Because the tweet itself, that one simple post, gave me more publicity than I could have dreamed of. It lit the fire under the whole campaign.

To this day, I often say a silent 'thank you' to Mr Fry. I don't know if he ever saw my reply. I don't know if he remembers tweeting about that weird poster with the lad grinning like a lunatic outside a mattress shop but things just kept getting bigger from there.

Paul kept the momentum going with more videos. We turned a little space at the back of the Pearse Street shop into a makeshift green screen studio. I was flying on mattresses like I was Aladdin, dressed up like a lunatic, doing daft skits. I was fully aware I was making an eejit of myself, but I didn't care. People loved it.

Irish-made mattresses at unbeatable prices became my unique selling point. The brand started to gain serious traction after we went viral. I began to notice a steady increase in sales. It didn't happen overnight, but the growth was consistent. We could see the momentum building, and it was clear the business was heading in the right direction.

Then came the mattress costume. A big foam suit shaped like a bed, complete with my grinning face printed on it. A friend of mine, Brian Traynor, was the man inside the mattress.

He'd wander the streets, waving at cars, chatting to passers-by like some LSD-tripping mascot. People loved him. He got honks, selfies and laughs. It was a ridiculously simple idea that worked so well.

We wrapped cars in yellow and red and put my picture on the side. They were like mobile billboards. We'd park them in high-traffic spots – this was great free advertising. People would see them everywhere, but we only had a few active. Even the radio got involved, doing a competition to guess how many Mattress Mick cars I had. It was just three at the time, but people thought there were more because we kept moving them around. The illusion worked. But Paul and I knew we needed to go bigger. 'We need a song,' I said, 'a proper Mattress Mick anthem.' Something catchy – so we set to work on making it happen.

We brought in Sean Mooney, a director, to help shoot the music video. Only problem? Paul wasn't too thrilled. Cue a bit of creative tension. One said this, the other said that, like two lads arguing over who gets to drive the clown car. I tried to play peacemaker and told them they could both work on it. Let's just say artistic differences were abundant.

We recorded the song first – 'Back With a Bang'. I brought in a couple of songwriters, a singer ... and guess who was on lead vocals. They got to work and came up with an amazing song, not just a catchy tune, but a power ballad. I was impressed at how good it was. The main line, which I sang, went, 'I'm back, I'm back, I'm back with a bang, The undisputed king of mattress land!' It was a very catchy tune, you'd hear it once and be humming it in your sleep, but that's what we wanted. We wanted it to be something people couldn't get out of their heads.

I was in a recording studio. Me! Singing a rap about mattresses! Never in a million years did I think that would happen. But hey, they say you can't teach an old dog new tricks. I say, watch me.

Then came the video. We filmed part of it in Windmill Lane. Dancers! Lights! Me! I was dressed as the mad scientist from *Back to the Future*, crouched in a DeLorean that we rented for €1000 from a collector. It felt like some sort of fever dream.

We shot the rest in a pub called D1 on Capel Street where I came in dressed like a 1980s pimp, full red silk suit, matching hat. We did a shoot in a hairdresser's where I got my hair done, though let's be honest, my hair's already perfect as it is. Then came a scene that made me a bit uneasy. Paul brought in scantily clad lingerie models, rolling around on beds. 'Paul, we're selling mattresses, not fantasies!' He just grinned and said, 'Sex sells, Mick. Sex sells.' We compromised. I drew the line at a scene with three bare arses wiggling in a row that took up the whole screen. 'That's a no from me, Paul.' He gave in, grumbling, but respected the call. I wanted fun, not offence.

It was exhausting, exhilarating and borderline insane. But it was working. We were creating something completely different, something that no retailer in this country had done before. I was an online influencer before it was even a thing. Paul was in his element directing the video; you could tell he had a real passion for it. Sadly though, with the way the world works, I don't think there have been many movie makers from the inner city flats in Dublin.

And right before all of this kicked off, a filmmaker named Colm Quinn popped into the shop. He'd heard about the madness. He wanted to make a documentary. And me being me, I said yes. Why not?

While this was all going on, Paul was quietly carrying the weight of the world on his shoulders. He was going through a rough patch and was signing on at the time, barely scraping by. You're allowed to work one day a week, so that's what he did. He'd come into the shop on Pearse Street, give it his all for the day, helping me sell mattresses, filming content and posting social media ads, but behind that enthusiasm was a man who was struggling.

He had debts piling up, heavy ones. He was doing everything he could to keep his head above water. He was living in a tiny, cramped place with his partner and their two young children. I knew the pressure he was under. It was constant and it wore him down. And the stress at home was building. I could see it, even if he didn't say much. I think he poured so much of himself into the Mattress Mick project – not just for me, but to try and create a better life for him and his family – that I think that it maybe caused strain in his relationship. The world doesn't wait for dreams to come true or for a business to become financially healthy; people want to be paid, and banks don't wait long.

I tried to help where I could, but Mattress Mick was only just getting off the ground. I had debts of my own. We were both struggling in our own ways, trying to make something long lasting and financially fruitful, but we were a long way off yet. Through it all, Colm Quinn kept filming. He captured Paul in those raw, real moments: the heartbreak, the exhaustion. No filters. Just life.

The hype had been building for weeks. The teaser clips, behind-the-scenes photos and me teasing the lyrics on social media made people curious about what we were doing. Confused, maybe. But definitely curious too.

And then we dropped 'Back With a Bang'. The video went live on YouTube, and within hours, it was flying. Views shot up into the thousands. Comments were flooding in: 'You have to see this.' 'Mattress Mick is deadly!' 'We love Mattress Mick!' It was insane. There I was, dressed like a mad scientist from 'Back to the Future', flying around on a mattress, surrounded by dancers and flashing lights like I was headlining Electric Picnic.

Some thought it was hilarious. Some were completely baffled. But no one could look away. It was catchy, over-the-top and absolutely unforgettable. Suddenly, I wasn't just 'that mattress guy from the posters' I was Mattress Mick: mattress mogul, viral sensation, rapper.

Radio stations started talking about it. Local papers ran stories. The *Irish Times* even gave it a mention. People on the street were stopping me, quoting the lyrics, asking for selfies. One lad even said his toddler wouldn't stop singing it around the house. 'Back with a bang!' echoed through the streets of Dublin. I thought, *Jesus, I've gone from beds to banger tunes.*

It wasn't just a joke any more, it was a brand. A movement, nearly. Mattress Mick had gone mainstream. The video helped take things to a new level. It gave the character personality, humour and, most importantly, exposure. And deep down, as mad as it all was, I knew this was the moment it had all turned around. Maybe that was what all the hardship was for: God was preparing me for my resurrection as Mattress Mick.

From that day forward, Mattress Mick wasn't just a gimmick. He was a household name, well in Dublin anyway. And it all started with a rap song, a few mad ideas and the belief that you're never too old, or too ridiculous, to go viral.

Chapter 14

Mattress Men

In the midst of all the chaos, with the media swarming around us and the pressure mounting, Paul was quietly unravelling. He always seemed to carry a storm behind his eyes – troubled, restless, always searching for something he could never quite find. At that point, things in his personal life had reached a breaking point. His relationship, already strained and frayed at the edges, finally collapsed. They broke up, and just like that, he was left without a home.

I couldn't let him out on the streets: he was still my friend, and I cared about him. So I told him he could stay in the shop on Pearse Street. It wasn't much, just a tired old place filled with mattresses, but it was shelter. That's where he stayed most of the time. He wasn't short of a mattress to sleep on, of course, but it wasn't a home. It was cold, draughty, and it hadn't been touched up in years, not since my mother left – the place needed a complete makeover. I knew it wasn't right, not for someone trying to rebuild their life. But in a strange way, I think it gave him the breathing room he desperately needed.

Paul comes from a close-knit family, so I knew he had another support network around him. He was going through so much at once, it was like watching someone trying to swim against a tidal wave. And I wish, truly, that I could have done more. But back then, I was doing what I could, offering a place to sleep, a bit of work, and someone to talk to.

One thing about Paul that never wavered was his devotion to his children. Through the debt, the stress, the heartbreak, he never let that part of his life falter. No matter how chaotic things got, he was always there for them. He made sure to take them out, spend time with them, create happy memories in the midst of the chaotic time he was going through. He is a good father. He loves his kids fiercely. He was also deeply committed to trying to climb out of the hole he'd fallen into. He wanted to do better, to be better. Even when he was all over the place, even when things felt out of control, he was still trying.

As things finally began to improve on the business front, with Mattress Mick starting to gain some traction, my hope was that Paul would start working with me more regularly. But then something came to light, something I couldn't ignore. I discovered a few discrepancies that started to unravel the trust I had placed in him. Paul had sold a mattress to a friend and kept the money, with the intention of putting it back, but life doesn't really work like that – you're always chasing what's already gone. Taking from Peter to pay Paul, literally.

It broke me to confront him, but what hurt even more was the look in his eyes, the look of shame and guilt. We had a long, difficult conversation ahead. He was gutted. He apologised over and over and said he'd pay it all back and in fairness, he did. He was truly sorry, and I could see how deeply he regretted it. Desperate people make desperate choices. My heart couldn't help but go out to him, so we agreed to start anew with the promise that something like this would never happen again.

Eventually, we came up with a plan to work together that

suited us both, financially. The business was steady enough, and I felt he deserved the chance. He managed the Pearse Street shop, handled the website and social media. It gave him a bit of freedom, no one breathing down his neck. He thrived in that. He had space to be creative in the green room, filming silly videos, playing around with ideas. It brought him back and gave him the opportunity to turn things around.

After a while he got back on track and he met someone new. They're still happily together, which is lovely to see. Over the years, we've had our ups and downs, arguments, fallouts, especially over who really came up with Mattress Mick. But at the end of the day, he worked hard and he was paid fairly. We understand each other though we are so different.

I'm glad I gave him another chance, but it was easy to see the good in Paul. I didn't want him to just become another statistic, a man crushed by life, forgotten, struggling to raise his kids. I wanted to believe in something better for him. And I still do.

While all this was going on – the whirlwind that was the music video going viral, the sudden flood of media attention, the mad rollercoaster of emotions with Paul – there was another story unfolding in the background. One whose weight, at the time, I barely understood. The documentary. Every moment, every twist and turn, was being captured through the ever-watchful lens of Colm Quinn.

Colm was something else. He had a rare gift. He managed to make himself almost invisible, like a shadow moving quietly through the chaos. It didn't feel like we were being filmed. There were no big lights or barked directions. Just Colm, ever present, ever silent, observing and capturing everything. It was like he wasn't even there and that was his magic and skill. Because in his almost invisible presence, we were ourselves, unfiltered, honest and raw.

Sure, in the videos we were performing, acting the eejit, bringing laughs but underneath all the Mattress Mick antics, we were real and vulnerable. Colm somehow managed to catch it all. He documented not just the spectacle, but the reality behind it. The everyday goings-on, the ups and downs, the cracks behind the laughter.

He captured the good, the bad and the downright ugly. Especially between me and Paul. There were moments of joy, yes, but also real power struggles. Conflicts about direction, ownership, who was steering the ship, who built what. It was tense at times. The brand was growing, and so were the egos. But I had to remind myself and everyone else, I'm Mattress Mick. I am the character, the face, the heartbeat of this whole thing. If I step away, if I stop being Mattress Mick, the whole thing collapses. People lose their jobs and the dream fades.

The documentary initially was only meant to be about ten minutes long, but as Colm was filming, I think he got more than he bargained for and made a feature length documentary instead. The world of film and documentaries? That was all new to me. I thought Colm would just stitch a few clips together, add a bit of music, and we'd have a nice little home video to look back on. A kind of scrapbook of our journey from a silly idea to media attention.

But then I saw it. The finished documentary took my breath away. It was brilliant. I sat there in disbelief, watching our lives unfold on screen, completely floored by the way Colm had woven it all together. He had brought our vulnerabilities to life, our pain, our triumphs, our battles, without judgement. He made our chaos into something cinematic.

Paul, in particular, was incredibly brave. He didn't shy away from the hard stuff. He allowed Colm to film moments that I honestly thought he'd never agree to. Like the confrontation over the mattress sale to his mate and taking the money. That was a tough conversation. Emotions were high. And Paul, to his credit, let the camera roll. He wanted honesty and total transparency, which took courage.

That honesty, though, did create tension. The question loomed: who came up with Mattress Mick? Who was really behind the brand? When I was interviewed, I spoke as myself, as Mattress Mick, and naturally the focus was on me. That's who the TV and radio stations wanted to talk to. I did acknowledge Paul's contributions, his marketing ideas, his social media wizardry, but maybe not enough in his eyes. It wasn't deliberate and at times I felt that I was being painted as the bad guy, but I understood the story had to be told. But that sting, that sense of being sidelined, was captured too. Nothing was left out. The film was entitled *Mattress Men*.

You think you know your own story, but you don't, not until you see it played back. Watching Paul's journey was heartbreaking. He was shown at his most raw, dealing with debt collectors, fighting to make ends meet and juggling fatherhood. It was touching, real and deeply moving. Colm didn't dramatise it. He didn't need to – the reality was powerful enough.

And then came the shock of all shocks: the film was nominated for an IFTA.

An IFTA! I couldn't believe it. Here we were, a Mattress Man and his mate from Dublin, up for nomination with films like *Bobby Sands: 66 Days, Atlantic, It's Not Yet Dark*. What a journey, from staring into the bottom of a pint glass, wondering what tomorrow would bring, to walking a red carpet. It was like living in a dream you didn't know you had or wanted.

The night of the IFTAs was unforgettable. We all suited up – Paul, Colm, Brian Traynor (our legendary man in the mattress suit) and me. Full black tie, the works. We weren't expecting anything. We were just proud to be there. When they read out the nominees for the George Morrison Feature Documentary Award, we were clapping, cheering the others on. And then, Miriam O'Callaghan, who was presenting the awards, said it.

'And the winner is … *Mattress Men*.'

We erupted. My God, we'd won an IFTA. We were on top of the world. Colm and Paul went up to accept the award, and I couldn't have been prouder. All the late nights, the arguments, it had all been worth it. Colm Quinn, that quiet genius with the invisible camera, had taken our messy, beautiful, chaotic lives and turned them into something that moved people, that meant something. He's not just a director, he's a magnificent storyteller. We're still friends to this day. Every now and then we'll meet for a pint in Clontarf.

I'll always be grateful to him. For seeing us. For telling our story. For giving Mattress Mick a legacy beyond the mattresses.

After the IFTA award and the viral sensation of the music video, life just became an endless stream of radio appearances, TV appearances, charity events, being invited to everything. Life was insane. There wasn't a night where I wasn't doing something or at some event making appearances alongside Brian Traynor in the mattress costume. It was great fun. I loved every second of it. I love having a laugh.

The documentary was produced by EZ Films and Faction Films, and the distributor was Element Pictures Distribution. They must have done a great job, because somehow we were nominated for an award at the Hot Docs Film Festival in Toronto.

Thanks to some help from Culture Ireland, which contributed towards travel, off we went to Canada. Paul, Brian and me, as well as Colm and his crew were able to go over. The film was screened three times: at the TIFF Bell Lightbox to a full house; at the University of Toronto; and at the oldest standing movie theatre in Toronto, the Revue Cinema. We didn't win the award but we had an incredible time, exploring the city, soaking up the atmosphere and getting a glimpse of a completely different side of life. Not bad for a boy from the wrong side of town. People genuinely loved the film and us – sure, who doesn't love the Irish? We felt like we'd truly arrived. I've also recently heard that, nearly ten years on, the film just sold in Japan. Who knows, we might be off there next.

We were becoming very well known, especially here in Ireland. I love people coming up and taking selfies. I never get sick of it. I'd never say no to anyone. It's a testament to all the hard work.

And people knowing who you are means that they've got what you're doing out there. It means you've done a good job, and I'm so grateful for that. I never understand why people get annoyed when someone asks them for a selfie. Why push yourself out in the public so much if you don't want to engage with them?

I was enjoying it. The business was doing well, and we were starting to look at opening some more mattress shops around the country. I still had lots of ideas. I wasn't resting. I wasn't saying, right, now we've done it. I was still open to new ideas. I was still wanting to grow and do different things.

In 2013 things had finally started to settle and get onto an even keel. But there's always something. Around 11 o'clock on the night of 7 October I got a phone call. It was a guy called Alan Fitzgerald. I picked up, not expecting anything unusual. But what he said stopped me in my tracks.

'Mick, I hear your shop is on fire.'

'What?' I said. 'What are you talking about?'

I hadn't heard a word about it. No calls, no alarms, nothing. But Alan had seen it on social media. Apparently, someone had posted 'Mattress Mick is on fire.' I thought it was a joke at first. Or a marketing stunt someone had taken too far. But it was very real.

Moments later, I was scrambling to find my keys and head over to the Coolock shop. As I pulled up in my car, I couldn't believe what I was seeing. There were flames bursting everywhere. It gave me the fright of my life. The fire brigade was on its way. It's a mad world we live in when the news reaches Facebook before it reaches the emergency services.

Still, no official word had come through. It turned out that the fire had started in the unit next to mine. From what I was told later, someone had broken into that building with the intention of setting it alight. They used petrol to make sure it burned fast and hot.

Unfortunately, that fire didn't stay contained. The flames spread quickly and caught on to our building too. And to make matters worse, we had a pile of old mattresses stacked outside, ready to be taken away for recycling. Naturally, they went up like kindling. Suddenly, rumours began flying that we'd put those mattresses out there on purpose to 'fan the flames'.

I couldn't believe what I was hearing. Why would I ever want to set fire to my own business? It was absurd. But once that kind of accusation is out there, it sticks. Mattresses can catch fire quickly, so there were accusations that I shouldn't have been storing them there, and that they should have been taken to the dump earlier. But these were old mattresses, and I had always stored them in that spot without any issues. I had every right to keep them there.

People love a scandal, even if it's completely baseless. The damage to our shop wasn't a total disaster, thankfully, but it was serious. We lost a lot of stock, mostly because of the smoke. Once a mattress is smoke damaged, it's worthless, you can't sell it, can't donate it, can't do anything with it. And we couldn't get into the building for several days, which meant lost time, lost sales and a lot of stress.

What made the night even more eventful was that RTÉ happened to be filming a documentary series called *Firefighters* at the time. So not only did the fire brigade show up, hoses in hand, but they had a full camera crew running behind them, filming every moment of the chaos. My business, going up in smoke, caught on national television. Anything I touch seems to attract attention, sometimes wanted, sometimes not.

We were lucky, though, the fire brigade arrived quickly and acted even faster. If it weren't for them, the entire building might have been reduced to rubble. The walls were already cracked from the heat, and the inside was a blackened mess. But they saved it. And most importantly, nobody was hurt.

Of course, the nightmare didn't end there. The aftermath dragged on for years. There were legal battles, insurance headaches, and questions we couldn't answer. We ended up in court, can you believe that, even though we had nothing to do with starting the fire. It took nearly 12 years for the whole thing to work its way through the system. Sometimes this country wrecks my head.

There were counterclaims, cross-examinations, wild theories, every trick in the book to muddy the waters. Thankfully, the courts eventually ruled in my favour, confirming that I had the legal right to store the mattresses where I did and that there was no wrongdoing on my part. In the end, it just felt like people were desperate to find someone to blame and I was an easy target. I swear on the Bible, on everything I hold dear, I would never, ever do something so stupid or reckless.

Still, it was a heavy blow. We were just finding our feet again after a rough patch, and the fire set us back a bit. No insurance pay-out, loads of lost stock, and months of cleaning up. And we never did get a straight answer about what really happened next door. There are whispers, rumours, conspiracy theories, but no solid answers.

What I do know is this: we survived. We picked up the pieces, brushed off the soot, and got back to work. And that's all you can do sometimes, as I have learned time and time again: keep going, even when everything around you feels like it's going up in flames.

And through all of this by my side was my beautiful wife Margaret, who supported me every step of the way, never faltering, never letting me down. She was so focused on being a mother. Being a mother to Margaret was everything. She adored her children. She doted on them. They were her pride and joy and she gave everything she had to them. And they are great girls. And we're so, so proud.

Life for a change was all on the up. Everything was looking great. Paul was getting along in the shop and his life was brighter. We had more Mattress Mick vans made up with my face, of course, plastered all over them, making mattress deliveries all around the country. Things were going far better than we both ever imagined.

Meteor (now Eir) ran a huge Christmas ad campaign every year. I got myself into one of those commercials. And bit by bit, the name Mattress Mick began to stick. Joe Duffy, Ray D'Arcy and others were very supportive and had me on their shows. I even did a lip-sync battle against Cathy Kelly on live TV, pretending to sing 'Satisfaction' by the Stones – and I won!

Richie Kavanagh, the Irish singer-songwriter best known for the hit 'Aon Focal Eile', an Irish classic in my book, approached me to write a song about me. Of course, being the yes-man that I am, I was absolutely delighted.

He came into the shop in Coolock to record the song and film the music video, and he even brought a few lads dressed up as Oompa Loompas, it was absolutely hilarious! I'm still not entirely sure what the Oompa Loompas were about, maybe it was his way of saying that I'm to mattresses what Willy Wonka is to chocolate!

The lyrics went:
'Two things in life you can't go without,
sure I heard it from my mother,
A good pair of shoes and a nice new bed,
If you're not in one, you're in the other.'

Chapter 15

Apollo House

While things were going well in my business and Mattress Mick was becoming a household name in Dublin, the city itself was facing serious challenges. Those in power seemed to be prioritising profit over the welfare of the people. Homelessness was at an all-time high, and many people were struggling in ways they never had before. This was getting impossible to ignore, unless you were a TD.

At this time the government had started a regeneration project in Ballymun on the northside of Dublin, which involved demolishing high-rise apartment blocks, with a promise from the government to replace them with modern homes, integrated into a community development plan that would benefit everyone in the area. That promise was broken. As a result, many residents were either forced to relocate or left without homes entirely. The neglect of this project caused the community and the area to suffer deeply.

What had happened in Ballymun was a contributing factor to the country's housing crisis. It was a housing emergency unlike anything Ireland had seen before. At the time, there were 3,607 people in emergency accommodation, 887 of whom were children. We thought that to be a national disgrace.

Filmmaker, activist and community worker Dean Scurry, a native of Ballymun, witnessed the devastation first-hand

and felt compelled to act. He approached musician Damien Dempsey to help him create a movement so revolutionary and impactful that the government would have no choice but to take notice.

Damien was just as passionate about the issue and the damage it was causing to so many, so he was more than willing to get involved. Dean then reached out to other influential figures in the arts and activism community, including musician Glen Hansard, who joined as a strong supporter, along with film director Jim Sheridan, actor John Connors and filmmaker Terry McMahon.

They all came together for a big meeting at the Axis Arts Centre in Ballymun, joined by members of the local community. Activist Brendan Ogle, a prominent Irish campaigner, was also brought on board.

Together, this group of people with a will of iron brainstormed ways to confront the crisis. One idea they floated was to occupy the GPO, though that didn't gain traction; if anything, it brought home the enormity of what might transpire from this. Eventually, after much discussion, they decided to take over one of the many vacant office buildings in the city centre: Apollo House.

Ironically, Apollo House had once been a social welfare office. Now, it would become a powerful symbol in the fight to raise awareness about the homelessness crisis, an issue that has always been close to my heart, especially after seeing it up close for many years working on Pearse Street.

There are countless vacant buildings across the city, offices sitting idle, completely unused, while people sleep on the streets, exposed to the elements and constant danger. To me, that's madness. We have the resources, we have the space, yet bureaucracy and red tape are treated with more respect than human dignity. That logic has always baffled me. People are quick to judge those without homes. I've lost my home, and I will never forget the loneliness and the insurmountable stress that caused me.

The plan was bold: to reclaim Apollo House, a NAMA-managed office block in the heart of Dublin city centre and turn it into a safe space for the homeless to live. One day, I got a call out of the blue from Dean Scurry. He told me about the project, what he and his friends were planning to do, and asked me to help by providing mattresses for the homeless to sleep on while they were staying in Apollo House. It sounded insane, unhinged, a big risk – so I was in.

I was absolutely delighted to be involved. I knew this was something radical, but it was a radical situation. Something bold had to be done, and this was it. The project became known as Home Sweet Home. Dean called me in December 2016, just two or three days before the occupation and I quickly got to work. I arranged for 40 single beds to be delivered to Apollo House. We packed the vans and parked them discreetly on Pearse Street, just around the corner. At 11 o'clock on a cold Thursday night in December, we zoomed over to Apollo House with the mattresses.

It felt like something out of an action movie. As soon as they got inside the building (I'm still not sure if they had keys or got in another way), they rang me and gave me the green light: 'Go, go, go!' We raced around the corner with the vans. The password to get into Apollo House was 'Midnight at the Oasis.' As soon as it was said, the gates opened and we were in, unloading the mattresses. It was chaotic, but we got them in.

Being in a position to help with that movement after my own struggles was something I was truly honoured to do and be part of. When people come together to help others with no ulterior motive, just to help, it's a powerful thing. It wasn't about money or publicity. It wasn't even about doing the right thing; it was about recognising housing as a basic human right, and, unlike those in power, doing something to help people access it.

What happened inside Apollo House was nothing short of remarkable. Volunteers from all walks of life came together and transformed that empty office block into a real home. The individual offices became bedrooms, offering privacy, warmth and safety to people who had been living on the streets. The canteen became a kind of recreation centre, a communal space where people could eat, relax, talk and just feel human again.

And it was all done with care and respect. The place was very well run. There was a strict no drugs or alcohol policy, which created a safe and stable environment. It was mayhem, but it was community. They got one Christmas there. Many great Irish musicians showed up and performed for the residents on the roof of the building, including Glen Hansard, Hosier and Kodaline.

On that Christmas Day, I went over with Margaret. The atmosphere was wonderful. They had the place beautifully decorated; you could smell the turkey cooking, and the singing rang through the air. The joy, the music, the sense of togetherness was overwhelming. You could start to feel hope in the air.

That hope, the feeling of some kind of triumph was short lived. They were only in Apollo House for 28 days before the

High Court issued an eviction notice. It was deemed illegal trespassing and declared unacceptable by the authorities. But somehow, they skipped the part where letting people die on the streets is acceptable. Excuse my French, but it's fucking disgraceful.

Of course, there was plenty of criticism surrounding the movement, as there always is when someone dares to raise their head above the parapet. People claimed it was all for show, that the homeless were being exploited for personal agendas, that it didn't achieve anything, or that it was just a grab for publicity.

Apollo House shone a light on a crisis the government had been ignoring. It gave dignity, shelter and solidarity to people who needed it most and, above all, it got people talking. Many of the residents of Apollo House were offered long-term accommodation, which is an achievement in itself.

Sometimes, my own country breaks my heart. We thought the problem was bad in 2017 when this happened, but today in 2025, the number of homeless people in Ireland has risen to 15,580. When I walk around my home city and see all the tents lined up along the Liffey, it's like walking around the set of some apocalyptic, surreal Netflix series. I feel a deep sense of shame about that. As one of the wealthiest countries in the world, surely we can do better. If I were part of the government, I would be so embarrassed. How have we let it come to this? I truly don't understand.

Even as a young boy growing up on Pearse Street, when people literally had nothing, you would never see people sleeping out on the streets like you do today. The world in 2025 feels like an unwell place. So many people are displaced and disenfranchised. I pray every day that this is part of a healing journey and that one day we will have leadership, not just in this country but all over the world, that truly cares about its people. That values the sanctity of all human life. That nurtures and protects, not exploits and lies.

It was an honour to be part of Home Sweet Home, and it's genuinely one of the most meaningful things I've ever been asked to be part of. What everyone involved achieved in such a short space of time was inspiring. It proved what's possible when people truly come together with heart, purpose and a bit of courage. Apollo House wasn't just a protest, it was a statement. A reminder that compassion still exists. And I was proud to be part of it.

Chapter 16

In Memory of Margaret: Wife, Mother, Matriarch

There are so many words I could use to describe Margaret: beautiful, fierce, loving, loyal and, yes, wonderfully bossy. When Margaret entered the room, you knew. It wasn't just her voice or her presence. It was an energy, a life force that swept through like a warm, unstoppable breeze. She had a way about her that made people laugh, that made them feel heard and seen. Margaret didn't need much to be happy, just her dog Poppy by her side and a good walk through Clontarf, where she knew everyone and stopped for chats. She always brought her own flask of coffee with her. As she said, the coffee from the coffee shops was too expensive and she refused to buy it. Even when we had a bit of money, she was still sensible like that.

She had a wicked sense of humour and loved a good laugh more than anyone I know. And when she laughed, it was full-bodied, real and infectious – a bit like my own mother's. She had this sparkle in her that could lift the darkest room. We had so many, many laughs over the years.

Margaret got on brilliantly with my sisters. She was in and out of their houses like a whirlwind. She'd spot an ornament or something shiny and say, 'Oh I like that, I think I'll take that home with me,' and off she'd go, claiming it without a thought. No one minded. That was just Margaret. Everything was shared, everything was borrowed and returned, eventually. There was no ownership among family in Margaret's book and she would be the same if anybody came to our house and saw something they liked. She'd hand anyone anything and not even think about it.

She was a devoted wife. Through the tough times, she never faltered. She knew how to stretch a meal, stretch the petrol in the car, and she'd also stretch love and laughter when there wasn't much else. I can still see her at the kitchen counter, calculating how far the car would get her. Her main concern was to reach Nolan's in Clontarf for the weekly shop. She was sharp, frugal, but never mean. Always generous in spirit, always giving more than she had.

Margaret wasn't exactly Delia Smith in the kitchen, but we were always well fed. She was more tinned soup than crab bisque, but that didn't matter to us. When we first moved in together and my side of the family was coming over for dinner, she was desperate to impress my mother, Catherine. Margaret thought they were a bit well-to-do and got very nervous about it. I told her not to worry, but she was getting anxious over everything.

She was making a big Sunday chicken roast dinner, which she found stressful even at the best of times. Now, I don't even know how it was possible, but somehow, she cooked the chicken upside down. The table was set, and everyone was waiting for their dinner. Margaret, already anxious, pulled the chicken out of the oven and it was nearly raw. Whatever way she had put it in, it just hadn't cooked properly.

We had a house full of hungry people and she was mortified. She had to come in and explain to my family, mostly my mother, who she was especially nervous about, that we'd have to do without the chicken because it wasn't cooked. I think we ended up eating some ham with the vegetables instead. We all just laughed about it, much to Margaret's relief. She never forgot it. It became one of those stories that got told again and again at family dinners … the tale of the uncooked chicken.

Margaret had a great sadness in her own childhood, but she rarely spoke of it with bitterness. Her mother passed away when she was very young. She was raised by her father until he got married again, to a lovely lady called Chrissie, who was a wonderful stepmother to Margaret. We all have very fond memories of her. Margaret's father and Chrissie had more children together. When Margaret was younger she spent Saturdays at her aunt's on Gardiner Street. She enjoyed the bit of fuss that was made over her; it was a break from responsibility as she'd often help look after the other children when she was at home.

She had a deep, unshakable love for her family, especially her father. That bond was sacred. And when Michelle came into the world, that protective love poured over into motherhood. Michelle and Marina were her girls. God help you if you said the wrong thing or gave either of them a funny look, Margaret would have you out the door.

The funny thing is Michelle speaks differently than us. No inner city accent. We don't know where she got the more elocuted speaking voice from. Margaret always laughed about that. Margaret had a thick inner city Dublin accent.

When Michelle went to Trinity to study Business, Economics and Social Studies, it was a whole new world to us. We weren't from that background. It was two different worlds. Michelle would bring her college mates to our house and Margaret would stress. She'd want it all to look nice. She didn't want to let Michelle down, so she'd run to Mary's, borrow plants for the garden, and make sure the house looked the best it possibly could.

Michelle's friends loved it. They liked how relaxed and welcoming it was. All the worry was for nothing. But still Margaret would call Mary: 'They're coming! Help me fix the place!' Mary would arrive, arms full of plants. It became a running joke.

Our Michelle always had a hunger for knowledge. As a child she was very funny too, always joking, and doing impressions, she'd have us in hysterics. She loved the stage and dancing. I thought she might have gone into acting but she chose psychotherapy instead.

When Michelle was small we would leave her with one of my sisters while we were away, and she'd fret. Always worried about where we were, how we were travelling and if we'd be safe. She'd ring six or seven times a day, just checking in. She was a worrier, but that is a Flynn family trait. Michelle met her husband very early on in life. After Trinity, they travelled to Thailand, Australia, all the usual post-graduation destinations. They had a great time. I even visited them in Australia with Marina and Margaret. Even though I hate planes, I'd do it to see my Michelle.

We were over the moon the day Michelle told us she was going to get married. We really liked her husband-to-be and knew he would be a wonderful partner to our girl.

Michelle got married on 7 July 2017 in St Patrick's Church, Killiney, a place that held deep meaning for us. That's where Margaret and I had gotten married, so to see Michelle get married in the same church was incredibly special. Even more meaningful was the fact that her new husband's grandad had designed that very church. It made the day all the more sentimental for both families.

Bouncing Back

It was a beautiful, sunny day, and I was determined to make sure Michelle had the perfect wedding. We had rented a stunning house out in Wicklow for the occasion. My job that morning was to make tea and toast, and put on a few rashers, making sure everyone was fed and ready for the big day.

As a surprise, I arranged for a Rolls-Royce to take Michelle to the church. Originally, a friend was going to pick us up to save a bit of money, but in the end, I couldn't resist surprising her with something truly special. Sitting in the car with Michelle, I was so nervous. I just wanted everything to be perfect for her. She looked absolutely stunning, and I was so proud of my girl.

Walking her down the aisle, I wasn't sure who was more nervous, me or her. I held onto her so tightly. It was one of the proudest, most emotional moments of my life, one that I will treasure forever. Everyone we knew was there, friends going back years. It was amazing to see how much love and support Michelle had around her on her wedding day. I had to give a speech too. Even though I'm used to public speaking, for some reason, I was completely overwhelmed with emotion that day and found myself unusually nervous. I just wanted to say the right thing.

I spoke about how Michelle reminded me of myself, how, as a little girl, she'd be riding her bike, struggling at first, but she never gave up. She kept going with such determination. That's always been her spirit and I think she gets that from me.

Margaret was wonderful too. She was beaming with pride – I'd never seen her so happy and joyous. At the same time, she was on high alert, making sure everyone was okay and having a fabulous day.

It really was a day we'll all remember forever. The next day at the rented house, Michelle and I were the first ones up, so we started cleaning up together. That gave us a lovely bit of father–daughter time, a quiet moment after the celebration.

A year later Michelle announced the news that she was expecting their first child. Margaret was over the moon. When Michelle's first child Daire arrived we were all overjoyed, and then not long after came Finn and of course our beautiful little Éabha arrived, each one more cherished than the last. Margaret spoiled them rotten. If they had a trampoline at home, they had to have one at ours, even if I'd gripe that it was uncalled for, forever the businessman. If Margaret could give them the world, she would've wrapped it up and handed it over. She was very protective of them too as she was her own girls. You wouldn't want to cross her. Especially when it came to her kids or grandchildren. That fire always came from love.

There are so many funny stories. So many little Margaret moments.

Like the time she babysat and snuck out back for a quick cigarette. When she heard someone coming, she didn't stub the cigarette out properly, shoved it in her coat pocket and ended up setting herself on fire. She came running out of the house like a mad woman, slapping at her coat, trying not to get caught. Or when she ruined Michelle's brand-new floors – she was trying to do a good deed and clean them, only to stain them permanently. In the end she blamed the floor guy instead, moaning about what an awful job he did.

As a father, one of my greatest joys has been watching the beautiful bond between my wife and our adopted daughter, Marina, grow over the years. It was in the little things, the everyday moments they shared together that brought most joy. They loved bringing out our dog Poppy for walks. Poppy was like our third child. We live not far from Clontarf Promenade, and that stretch of coastline became something of a ritual for the two of them, a place to spend time together and talk.

Most days, they would set off with Poppy eagerly bouncing around, ready to go. They always followed the same path: down to the baths and then further on to the slip, coffee in hand. I'd often stay back, giving them their space, this was their time. Sometimes I'd go along, and we'd end up in The Yacht sharing a bowl of chicken wings.

These aren't monumental memories or anything grand, but it's the little day-to-day moments you get used to over time, the ones you really miss. Like taking the dog out for walks and stopping for something to eat.

Margaret and Marina would always come back from those walks rosy-cheeked, laughing about what Poppy got up to and how she used to flirt with other dogs on her travels. Their bond deepened over the years, and it was beautiful to see.

There was one particular day when they took Poppy out and a storm rolled in unexpectedly when they were halfway along their usual route. I remember watching from the window as the sky turned that deep Dublin grey. I thought for sure they'd turn back. But no, not my Margaret and Marina. They wouldn't let a little thing like a storm stop them. The rain came down in sheets, the wind kept howling, and yet they kept going. When they finally got home they were soaked through and laughing like schoolgirls. You could see Poppy looking at them like they'd lost it as she shook herself dry.

The best parts of family life aren't built from elaborate gifts or perfect holidays. They're made from time spent together: a walk by the sea, a dog who refuses to go in the water, laughter in a rainstorm. Also, it's much cheaper. (Joke.) Now, as Marina becomes a woman and finds her own path in life, after everything we went through to get her, I'm filled with immense pride and joy.

One thing about Margaret was that she never cared about what anyone thought of her. She'd throw on any old thing and take the dog for a walk. She didn't give two hoots, but when she dressed up, my God, she looked absolutely stunning.

Whenever she was annoyed at me, I was always called Mr Flynn. And I could overhear her sometimes talking to my sisters, when it would be 'Mr Flynn' or 'your brother'. That's when I knew I was in trouble. I have many friends, and lots of them are women, and she never minded. I think, to be honest, that she was glad to get me out from under her feet. We trusted each other. And that trust was never broken. At the end of the day, we loved each other very much.

In November 2022, Margaret was complaining of a sore throat, and that's all we thought it was at the start. Margaret was never big on going to the doctor, but she'd make sure everybody else would go. That was just Margaret, making sure everyone else was all right, looking after others and putting herself last.

I was away in Spain, just for a little break and a little breather from the pressures of work with my friend Dennis Carroll. Margaret told me she was going to the doctor just to get checked out. I just thought they'd suggest some Lemsip or something and send her on her way.

I had just stepped in the door after coming back from Spain when she told me she wasn't well. She told me she was seeing a doctor and attending appointments at St James's Hospital. Then, almost as an afterthought, she said 'Michael, I've got cancer.'

Time just stopped. The world around me froze. I couldn't process anything else at that moment. It was like all the noise drained out of the room. For me, cancer has always been a word that means one thing: death. It was horrible. Truly horrible. They had found a growth in her throat. At first, I didn't think she understood the full weight of it. Margaret was always strong and resilient in a way that made you think she could take anything on. Brave, without ever making a fuss about it.

She didn't want to face the reality of what was happening. But I couldn't help but see how her energy was draining away slowly, her body shrinking. Watching it all unfold like a film that I couldn't pause or rewind.

When she told me, there were no tears. She didn't cry. Not once. She just … said it. Calm. Maybe too calm. I think a part of her was in denial. Or maybe she was just trying to protect us, like she always did. She said she had a 'growth,' like it was something they could just remove and she could carry on. But it wasn't. And I think she knew, somewhere deep inside, she just wasn't ready to say it out loud.

It rocked the entire family. We'd already been through so much. I'd lost Brian and Mary. And she'd lost her brothers, John and Noel, not long ago. All of this really upset Margaret and stressed her out because she loved us all so much. I think that was the cause of her hair falling out, the stress of it all. But I never imagined this coming, as quick as it did. That's one of my big regrets, that I wasn't with her when she got the news.

Margaret also got a hairpiece for the front of her hair because it was falling out so much. Even her teeth had started to fall out, but that's the reality of it. That's what this bastard of a disease does to you.

She became a bit of a recluse and hid away in her room. She stopped answering phone calls and didn't want anyone to see her, apart from me, Michelle and Marina, and her three sisters, Caroline, Christine and Sharon. We were the only people she'd let in. Even my sister Catherine, who she was very close to, she didn't want to see, which broke our hearts because it was so unlike her. She was such a people person.

By the time she got the diagnosis, it had gone too far. It was far too aggressive. She wasn't offered chemo or radiotherapy. It was just a question of controlling the pain as much as possible. Michelle and Marina did everything they could for her, as did I.

But it was horrific to see her like this. The more tests we had, the worse the prognosis got. There was no hope. It seemed there was no getting out of this one. One day I was sitting next to Margaret in the bed. By this time the cancer from her throat started going into her brain. So it distorted everything for her. Catherine arrived at the door, 'Catherine's here, would you like her to come in and see you?' I gently asked. She was adamant. 'No,' she yelled. She didn't want to see anyone. She just wanted to be left alone.

That was the moment I knew I was losing my Margaret. I came halfway down the stairs and my sister Catherine stood at the bottom. My heart just broke. I sobbed like a child. After all the loss and the pain, I didn't think I could take it any more. But Catherine was a solid rock. She was there for me throughout it. And for that, I'm ever so grateful.

It wasn't long before Margaret was admitted to St James's. Margaret's sisters, Caroline, Christine and Sharon, and my sister Catherine went with her. Not long after, a lady from the hospice arrived and said to Margaret, 'I need to talk to you and I need to tell you that you're a very, very sick girl. Do you want to know what's going to happen?' And Margaret replied, 'No. No, no, I don't want to know anything. Don't tell me a thing.' She was in denial about how sick she was. The lady in the hospice called out Margaret's sisters and my sister Catherine to talk to them about what was going to happen. I don't blame Margaret for not wanting to know. I think I would have been the same.

The lady from the hospice was saying Margaret would need to go there sooner than any of us could have imagined. When our girls were told, I think they were in denial. They said, 'No, no, she's just going in for recovery, to have a rest.' It just all happened so quickly, I can't blame anyone for not being able to comprehend it.

I'd spoken to the hospital previously, so I already knew what was going to happen. On Christmas Eve, Margaret was moved to St Francis Hospice in Raheny. It was one of the most heart-wrenching moments of my life. There's never a good time to bring someone you love into a hospice. It always feels final, even if you're trying to convince yourself it's just temporary. But Christmas Eve … that was something else.

I remember standing outside the hospice, nervously pacing, waiting for the ambulance to arrive. It was bitterly cold. The type of cold that gets into your bones, but I barely noticed it. My heart was thudding so loudly it drowned everything else out. And then the doors opened, and there she was my Margaret, frail, confused, bundled in blankets, being wheeled in by kind, soft-spoken paramedics who had clearly done this a thousand times before.

Christmas morning 2022 came far too quickly. There should've been excitement, wrapping paper, laughter echoing down the hallways of a house filled with family. Instead, I found myself walking the long, quiet corridors of the hospice, coffee in one hand, a lump in my throat I couldn't swallow down. When I saw her being wheeled through the ward in a chair, my chest physically ached. Her eyes were distant, clouded with painkillers, and though she didn't fully grasp where she was, somewhere inside, she knew it was Christmas.

There were no decorations, no carols playing, no sense of celebration. Just hushed voices, tired nurses and families like ours clinging to moments they feared might be their last. But Margaret was surrounded by love. That mattered most. Her sisters, Caroline, Sharon, Christine, and her brothers Eddie and Peter were there. Her brothers John and Noel, God rest them, had passed away a year or so before, and we felt their absence deeply that day. Still, the family rallied, each of us doing our best to hold it together.

I remember sitting by her bedside, her hand in mine, and feeling so utterly powerless. You keep hoping for a miracle, even when the doctors have told you exactly what's coming. You play mental tricks on yourself. We just weren't ready to face it. That kind of denial is a strange comfort, it gives you room to breathe, to survive one more day.

What got us through were the incredible staff at St Francis. The kindness and compassion they showed us touched us deeply, and we will be forever grateful for the comfort and dignity they gave Margaret in her final days. There were no visiting hours; we were welcome anytime, day or night. They brought tea, blankets, comfort and a calm presence that made a horrible situation a little more bearable. Nothing was ever too much trouble. You could see how much they cared, not just about the patients, but the families too. They treated Margaret with such tenderness. I watched how gently they spoke to her, how they adjusted her pillows or stroked her hand. They're angels, every one of them.

In the midst of all this sorrow, we tried to find small joys, things to keep her spirits up. Strangely enough, one of the only things she seemed to crave was McDonald's. She always loved hamburgers, no cheese, just ketchup and a pickle. So I'd nip out and bring her one, and sit by her bed while she took slow bites, smiling weakly, like it was the best thing in the world. It became our little ritual.

The hospice even let me bring her a small can of Carlsberg. I'd hand it to her with a wink, and she'd take a sip like it was champagne. It was these tiny moments of normality that gave us some peace. In a place where everything felt foreign and final, those burgers and beers were reminders that Margaret was still in there somewhere.

I was there as much as I could be, barely leaving her side. Her sisters were in and out, sharing stories, dabbing their eyes when they thought no one was looking. We all handled it differently. Some of us were quiet, others tried to keep things upbeat. But underneath it all was the same pain, the knowledge that we were working up to our final goodbyes.

Within a blink of an eye she became so fragile, almost like a little baby. Whatever drug she was on distorted everything. She'd pretend she was on the phone sorting things out with people. It's funny even in the midst of absolute heartbreak and devastation; there can be little moments of humour that just take you out of despair.

Those last few months of her life were the closest I'd ever felt to her. There was always deep love there, but we never showed it. We were never ones for massive displays of affection, but it was there and we knew it.

In the last few days of her life, she'd wear my big hat because she said she felt close to me and she could smell me on it. She used to wear it all the time. I was the only person she kept asking for. 'Where's Michael? When's Michael coming in? I want Michael.' My compassion overflowed for her, and we just wanted to be near each other as much as we could. She adored me, I knew that, and I her.

Then came the call. Four in the morning. That hour that always brings bad news. It was the end. Marina and I leapt out of our beds. I called some of the family, Michelle rang the others. We all started heading towards the hospice. When we arrived, we were told that she had taken a turn for the better and would see out the next day or two. I stayed until the next morning.

I spoke to the doctor, and he assured me that she'd be okay for the rest of the day. I had wages to pay at work, so I nipped into the office quickly. Life, as cruel as it can be, doesn't stop, even when your heart is breaking. Wages still need to be paid. I was on my way back when I got stuck behind a bus. The phone rang. It was Catherine. She told me I had to hurry. 'I'm doing my best,' I said. But it wasn't enough.

And then came the second call; Catherine again. When I answered I could tell in the silence and the delay in her voice that it had happened. As soon as Catherine said the words, 'Margaret has gone,' it felt like the world had crumbled around me. When you hear those words, it's like the strangest silence and everything seems to stop moving. You almost feel like you're not here, part of you has gone with them.

My Margaret, she was gone. I missed her by ten minutes. Ten minutes. She slipped away quietly, on her own terms. Everything was on her own terms. And I believe that she didn't want me to be there when she passed. She spared me that moment. I don't know if it was for her sake or mine.

The same thing had happened with Mary, Brian, my mother and with my father. I had wanted to be with all of them. I always try. But somehow, they slip away just before I arrive. I don't know, maybe they don't want me to see them go. Maybe they think it would be too hard on me. And maybe they're right.

When I got to the hospice my girls were heartbroken, as we all were. My emotions were all over the place, I couldn't comprehend that Margaret wasn't going to be there with me to see it all. It hit my daughter Marina especially badly, losing her Irish mother. It's almost like she's lost two mothers. Michelle was distraught. You feel helpless in moments like that, you wish there was something you could do to make it better for them. They were all so close and Margaret left a huge void that can never be filled.

It was 1 February 2023, St Brigid's Day, when she passed away. My beautiful, strong and funny wife is up in the big supernova in the sky. I know that she is watching over us.

Looking back now, I'm grateful for those days, as painful as they were. They gave us time. Time to show her how much she was loved. Time to hold her hand, brush her hair, sit in silence, or laugh softly about something silly. And most importantly, time to say goodbye, not with a grand gesture, just by simply being with her.

Christmas will never feel the same. There's a slight emptiness now where there used to be joy. But I also remember the love that filled that hospice room. The strength of our family. The kindness of strangers. The small comforts of a burger and a beer. And I remember Margaret's smile, faint but full of warmth, reminding me that even in the darkest moments, love remains.

On the day of the funeral, Saturday 4 February, Josephine McCaffrey – who would, of course, later go on to write this book that you hold in your hands – came and said a few prayers, and later, she sang at Margaret's graveside. Little did we know later that the vacant plot Josephine was singing on would become the burial place of Sinéad O'Connor five months later. My wife lies at rest next to the amazing Sinéad O'Connor. Margaret was always a massive fan of hers, and at least I know she is in good company.

I go up to visit Margaret at the grave often. There are always people around to visit Sinéad. Some extreme fans, some of them lying on top of her grave, which I find a bit disturbing.

It was only a couple of years ago that she passed and I still feel lonely. I still feel the heartache. I haven't gotten over her loss.

After Margaret passed, I knew deep down that I would never seek love in the same way again. There's something about losing the person who anchored your world – it shifts your whole sense of time, of self, of what's important. Though the grief softens over time, the emptiness and the loneliness never fully disappear. Margaret wasn't just my wife; she was the love of my life. The idea of anyone else filling that space feels not only impossible but unnecessary.

Chapter 17

Mattress to Matinee

Before Margaret became ill, there had been another development in my life, one that delighted Margaret particularly, and that was the musical about my life story. I'm always meeting weird and wonderful people, and this particular day was no different.

On a summer evening in 2019 I was at one of my local spots in town, Davy Byrnes. I usually go in there for a quiet pint after work. On this occasion, I was sitting outside, just about to leave, when this fella came up to me. He wanted to run in and use the toilet but he had a dog with him so he asked me if I'd look after his dog while he went to the loo. I had five minutes to spare so I sat there, holding the dog. I looked up to see a woman – Josephine McCaffrey – dressed as a potato. I said, 'What in the fuck are you doing?' She said she was promoting a comedy night in the Duke in her potato costume. It was called Laughter Lines Dublin, and she and her friends had formed a comedy troupe together. They had a weekly residency there so she was handing out flyers to everyone up and down Grafton Street.

She recognised me, handed me a flyer and said, 'You should come along to the show one night. You'll really enjoy it.' I said to her, 'You don't look like a potato, you look like a bollocks.' The potato outfit, you see, had the look of a certain part of a man's anatomy. She laughed; she could see it too.

In that moment I instantly took to her. I could see she was good fun and had a good sense of humour. I admired her tenacity, I probably saw something of myself in her, a little glimmer of what I'd do. She was willing to dress up like a complete idiot to promote something that she cared about. It endeared her to me instantly, and there was just something about her I liked. I took one of her flyers, and then I gave her my business card. I told her to contact me any time, if I could help with anything. She thanked me and that was that really. I didn't think anything of it. But being the tenacious woman she is, she called me a few days later. I think she was doing her best to try and do something on the comedy circuit in Dublin.

She wanted to know if I could maybe help with promoting the comedy show and to support it in some way. And she also wanted to do a few little comedy sketches for me. I always say yes to everything, so we got talking and over the next while we did some funny videos with her comedy crew, Declan McFadden, Grainne Boyle, Mark Hanratty and Sophie Merry. When I met them all I could see that they were a good bunch of people.

We did a few little bits together while she was concentrating on the other things that she was doing. It was later that I found out she was being ordained to be a reverend. I never would have thought this crazy woman dressed as a potato would be doing that! But everyone surprises you now and again. Getting to know her more, I found out that she was a writer, a singer and an actor, just an all-rounder really. She then wrote a few radio jingles for me as well. I believe a couple of the comedy troupe helped out with that.

Then one day, I got a call from her and she asked me how I would feel about doing a musical about my life story. Now,

I was a bit unsure at first, but over the years I have learned that nothing ventured, nothing gained. The power of yes has done me good so far. So I said yet another yes. And that was it. That was the start of the journey of writing a musical about my life.

Josephine told me that my life story was worth telling and that the colourful, mad moments would be great set to music. She was so enthusiastic and I could sense that she was a talented woman – mad, but talented. She wrote an amazing script, a script that depicted my life from the Pearse Street Boy days right up into the present.

She depicted my relationship with my mother, my heartbreaks, my journey with Paul, all of this was put into the musical. When I read the script I was overwhelmed. Every moment touched me. I was overjoyed with the work she'd done. So then the next part of the journey was getting it on its feet and finding the man to play me, Mattress Mick.

This was fun and got a lot of media attention. We went on the hunt for someone good-looking enough to play me. Josephine put the call out and we started the audition process.

Obviously doing something like this out of the blue will always add its own stresses to life. Because people can be judgemental, they can put things down. Lots of people thought it was silly, and others thought it was great, but I was well used to that at this stage of my life and I didn't care. I'm stubborn and if I want to do something, I'll do it and take little notice of what others say, but then I've always been like that.

All this work on the musical coincided with Margaret's illness. Josephine tried to convince me to put it off, but I was adamant that we should keep going. I needed the distraction.

Without it, I think I'd have gone mad. I know that's what Margaret wanted as well. She was so thrilled about the musical. I'd have loved her to have seen it. I kept talking to her about the musical and how excited I was about it. She was looking forward to seeing it too.

On 27 April 2023 the premiere of the musical came. The buzz was unbelievable. Nearly every radio station in the city interviewed me. I was on Morning AM, The Six O'Clock Show, RTÉ Radio, 104 FM … you name it, I was there.

The show was completely sold out. At the end the crowd went wild and we got a standing ovation. The energy in the room was electric. People came up to us saying it was one of the best nights out they'd had in years — fun, uplifting and full of heart. The feedback was touching. I could see it, this musical had legs. It could really go somewhere. Josephine wanted to go back to the drawing board afterwards to tweak, rewrite and refine things. It was her first musical, after all, but I thought she did an incredible job. And the best part? It's coming back soon. Honestly, it's just a brilliant night out. We even tried to get on *The Late Late Show*. Unfortunately, we didn't hear back. Maybe next time, Patrick Kielty?

The heartbreaking part was when I was in the theatre watching the show. I looked at the seat next to mine. Margaret should have been sitting there watching it with me, but she wasn't. In that moment, I felt her absence. It really kind of awakened me to what was lost. I know she would have loved it and it would have made her laugh. Maybe she was watching it from somewhere else.

Josephine was very supportive through all this time. She is one of the most mixed bag people I've ever met, but I think that's why she's, let's say, different. The reason she came back to Ireland was because her father got sick with cancer. She told me about the day her long-term relationship ended with a phone call. Just an hour later, her sister called to say their dad had been diagnosed with cancer, and it was serious. She said it felt like the Earth stopped moving. She came back to be with her dad and to look after him; to do what she could to help out while he was ill. Her father passed away very quickly after diagnosis. I think it took a while for her to get over it, but by the time I met her, she was dressed as a potato so things had improved. I know that experience knocked her life off course. That is how she somehow found herself in Dublin doing a comedy show. She understood what I was going through and was a support through that time.

Josephine has become a good friend through this and I think she knows my life story better than I do at this stage. And that will be there forever, that musical, a testament to my life. So I've had the documentary, I've had the musical, and now we're doing the book. Life is a crazy old game, but I'm still going to play it knowing that Margaret is close by somehow.

Chapter 18

I'm a Believer

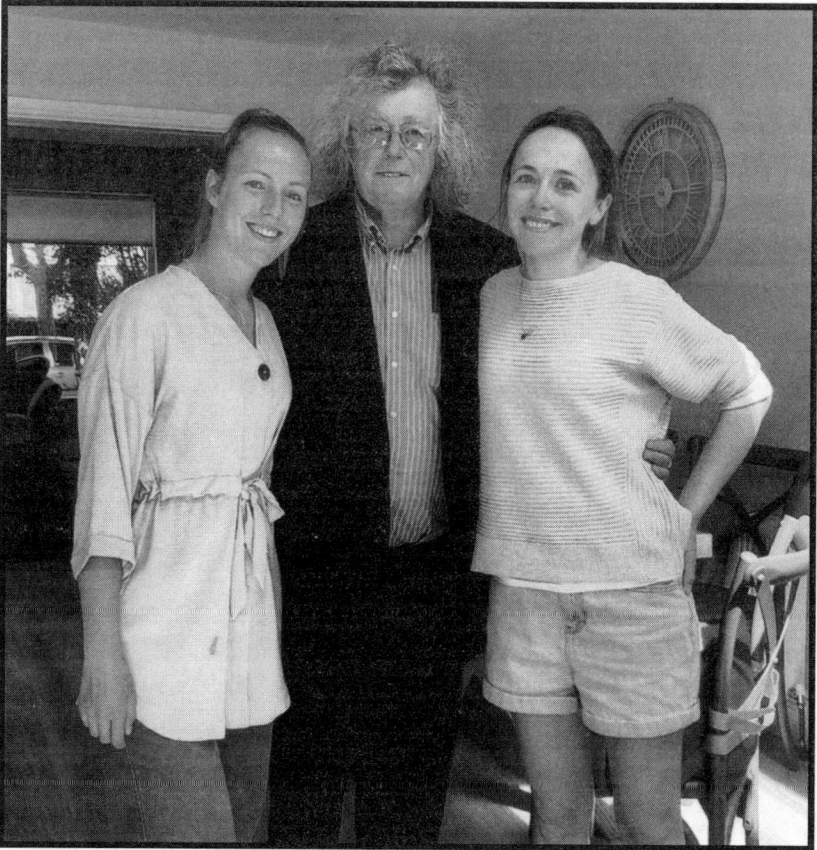

People ask me from time to time if I'd ever marry again. The answer is a firm no. I have no interest in settling down with anyone else. That chapter is closed, not out of bitterness, but because it was complete. Margaret and I had something special, and I don't believe you get that kind of love twice. But I'm not lonely. Far from it. I have a circle of great friends, many of them women, and I enjoy meeting new people all the time. I'm always out and about, having a cup of tea or going for a drink, sharing stories, having a laugh.

At this stage in life, I enjoy my own company more than ever. I've come to appreciate the simple moments, the freedom of doing what I like when I like. But that doesn't mean my life is dull, far from it. If anything, things have become madder and more unpredictable. I'm surrounded by wonderful characters, writers, singers, poets and businesspeople. I don't tolerate fools easily, never have, and I certainly don't have time for insincerity. I like to be around people who are honest and interesting, who challenge you in some way, who bring good energy.

You wouldn't believe the kind of characters I meet daily in the mattress shop. Some people walk in just to meet Mattress Mick, not even to buy a mattress. I get handed Christmas presents, homemade cakes, Easter eggs, you name it. I've had people refuse to buy a mattress unless I lie on it with them. But it has changed a lot since the pandemic. Less rolling about, more selfies. People love getting a photo of themselves lying beside me on a mattress, grinning like lunatics. I don't mind it. It makes people smile, and that's worth something.

But beyond the fun and chaos, there's a deeper side to all of it too. Amid the laughter, I've heard heartbreaking stories. People come in not just for a mattress, but sometimes because they have nowhere else to turn. One woman who came into the shop crying is especially memorable to me. She was living in a small apartment with her 11-year-old son. They had one single bed between them, and she didn't have the money to buy another. She was desperate but dignified. There was something about her story that touched me deeply.

She wasn't asking for a handout. She was doing everything she could to provide a decent life for her child, but it simply wasn't enough. And what could I do? I'm Mattress Mick. If I can't help a child get a good night's sleep, then what's the point? I gave her a bed. No questions asked. We delivered it to her home and it was clear her situation was genuine. No furniture, no luxury, just her and her son in a small one-bed flat trying to get by.

A few days later, she returned to the shop, beaming. She brought me a small box of sweets and a lottery ticket. That meant the world to me. It wasn't about the value of the gift, it was her way of saying thank you, a gesture filled with appreciation. That's the kind of payment I value most.

Outside of the shop, life never ceases to surprise me. I get calls to do the wildest things. Telly appearances, radio interviews, photoshoots. Just the other day, a photographer called Nina Val rang me up, asking if I'd pose in a bathtub, fully clothed with the shower raining down on me. She was doing a project on 100 well-known Irish personalities, including the Lord Mayor. And now, apparently, Mattress Mick. I believe I'm 43rd – not bad for a Pearse Street boy.

Life is for living. If there's a bit of craic to be had, I'm in. I'll wear a hat in the bath with the shower raining down on me if it makes someone smile.

Among all the sadness, I've had great joy in my life as well. I have many stories to tell; I have made many friendships; I've had mad adventures, and very meaningful moments with ones I hold dear. I've seen how giving someone a bed can change their life. I've rolled around on mattresses for laughs. I've shared tears and tea in the same hour. That's the beauty of it. Life is chaotic and wonderful. And as long as I have the strength, I'll keep saying yes to all of it.

I wouldn't change a thing. Not a single thing in my life. Sure, there were times I felt cheated, let down and incredibly lonely. But I know now that the path I was sent on, it had a purpose. It's helped people along the way.

When my dad died, I was just 19. I had to step up and take care of everyone. But everything that happened, every high and low happened for a reason. I didn't always see those reasons at the time, but looking back now, I understand, it all makes sense.

There was a reason I opened the shops that succeeded, and the ones that failed so drastically. A reason Margaret came into my life. Back then, I'd often find myself asking, 'Why is this happening?' But you only see the bigger picture years later. Like when I had to liquidate the furniture businesses after 26 years of hard work. I couldn't wrap my head around it at the time. But now, I see it as part of the journey.

All the ups and downs shaped who I am, and I'm grateful for it.

I've looked after people, and people have looked after me. I still don't understand why my sister and brother were taken before me. I'm the eldest, and yet I'm still here. But I believe this is the path that God laid out for me.

You would think, after the horrific time I experienced with the Christian Brothers, that I would have turned my back on the Church entirely, that I'd be bitter, angry, resentful towards all things connected to religion. Many people who suffered under institutions like that turned their backs on the Church, and understandably so. But for some reason, deep inside me, my faith remained untouched. Despite everything, I never let my experiences shake my belief in God.

I always had faith. It wasn't something taught to me, it was something that simply lived in me, a quiet knowledge that no cruelty from men could undo. Sure, over the years I came to disagree with plenty about the Catholic Church, the hypocrisy, the corruption, the shameful cover-ups. There is much the institution must answer for. But my relationship with God, my personal faith, has always remained unbroken. It has been the one constant in my life, my greatest source of strength through the storms.

Whenever I have a moment, I would slip into a church, sit quietly in a pew, and just be. No grand prayers, no requests, just silence and presence. I found such peace there, surrounded by the smell of candles and whispered hopes.

Every Sunday, I made it my business to take Mam to Mass when she was with us. We attended the Immaculate Heart of Mary Church on City Quay, where she met my father and it became a special part of my life. I wasn't just attending; I was involved. I would often read at Mass, standing up before the congregation, lending my voice to the service. Those mornings grounded me.

Having God in my life is something I hold very dear. Especially during moments of profound loss, losing my loved ones, it was then that I felt the divine closest to me. It's strange how grief draws you nearer to something bigger than yourself. In those raw moments, God wasn't just a distant, invisible figure in the sky. He was right there beside me.

I firmly believe there is something greater than us. Always have. I can't for a moment believe that this life, this incredible, intricate world, was just the product of a random explosion and blind chance. No, there has to be more. There has to be a 'before the beginning', a divine story written into our existence.

I also firmly believe in life after death. I don't know what form it takes, whether it's heaven as the pictures paint it, or something even more beautiful beyond imagining, but I know, deep down, that death isn't the end.

I believe our loved ones are still with us. I feel their presence often, sometimes stronger than the living people around me. I still connect with them when I'm alone. And sometimes, somehow, I feel they answer. Not in words, but in feelings, in small signs.

I named my father the chairman of my company. I truly believe he's still guiding me, supporting me from wherever he might be. I believe we can connect with the people we've lost. I still connect with Margaret, and I feel like she answers me back. Maybe it's just in my mind, but it feels real to me. It brings me comfort.

I believe in the power of prayer, in hope and in myself. Margaret was always proud of Mattress Mick, even if she didn't love the public attention. She didn't understand why people wanted selfies with me. To her, I was just Michael Flynn, the fella she knew for years.

Margaret and I used to go into town at Christmas with cash in €5 notes and just hand them out to the homeless. We didn't always have much, but when we did, we gave it. People would call out, 'Here come Mr and Mrs Mattress!' Margaret loved that.

Margaret and I never forgot where we started or what it was like to struggle. We knew how tough life could be for people, and that understanding stayed with us. No matter how far we'd come, we always tried to keep our hearts open to others.

So, what's the meaning behind it all? Why did I pull through when so many others didn't? I don't know. But now I've told my story, and I hope it helps someone out there. I never really planned to tell it, not even to the people closest to me. But now feels like the right time.

If you asked me who I'd thank, I'd start with my wife. She stood by me through the good times and the bad. Our relationship didn't start in the most traditional way, but that's just part of our story. Part of the plan. We've got our daughters, Michelle and Marina, and none of it would've happened without all the other pieces falling into place.

I've always been ambitious. Always wanted to be successful. That's why failure hit me so hard when it came. When the furniture business collapsed, it was devastating. But even then, I told myself: I may have failed, but I'm not a failure. A lot of it was outside my control, economic changes, the country's situation at the time. I picked myself up and kept going. I didn't fall into bad habits, I didn't give up. I stayed resourceful.

Truthfully, I think I thrive on problems. I've had so many that I just learned how to handle them.

If you were to ask me whether I had any regrets, the answer would be no, not really. I just wish I had been 15 years younger when Mattress Mick started. I was 60 when I registered the name. Most people start businesses in their thirties or forties. But I reinvented myself at 60. And that just shows you, it's never too late. You're never too old. No matter what society tells you, you can start something new at any stage in life.

Mattress Mick only launched in 2012 but people think it's been around forever. That says something. It feels like it's woven into a part of Dublin culture. I've even been called a cult figure a few times, and you know what? I'll take that.

When it comes to my girls, I just want to leave them comfortable when I'm gone. I don't want them to go through the struggles I went through. Marina is doing great. She works with me now and is brilliant with technology, which is a huge help to me. She's got potential to do great things. She's also interested in photography and has a passion for it. I think that is the route she will take. And if I'm not around, I know Michelle will guide her. Michelle's amazing too. She's got her own business, she's a psychotherapist, working in perinatal mental health. She's a devoted mother and wife. I couldn't be more proud of them both.

Meanwhile, I will keep making an eejit of myself to pay the bills. Mind you, I've had a few run-ins with the law, maybe more than a few, over the years, mostly for flyers and plastering myself all around Dublin without permission. When we launched our guerrilla marketing campaign, we put posters up all over Dublin, empty shops, empty signs, anywhere we could. It worked. People noticed. Dublin County Council, however, weren't thrilled. They called it 'littering' and kept sending me fines.

I never paid one of them. I went to court over 35 times and always defended myself, no solicitor. I'd stand up and say, 'All I'm trying to do is get my business off the ground. This isn't litter. I'm not causing any obstruction or danger.' Most judges struck it out. One judge called me litter. I looked her in the eye and said, 'I'm not litter, I'm Mattress Mick.' That judge let me off and later got herself a good deal on some bedroom furniture. Eventually, I became friendly with the inspectors. They were only doing their job. But that campaign helped people learn about me and it helped save my brand.

I often go into universities to give talks to young students about business, its potential, the pitfalls, and the reality of building something from nothing. I share my journey, including the mistakes, the risks, and the lessons I've learned along the way.

As well as universities, I've also visited prisons to give talks and share my experiences. We're now looking at performing some of the songs from the musical for inmates. I was recently asked about this on the radio: why would I bring entertainment to people who've committed crimes? The argument goes, such people they don't deserve it, they have done bad things and are in prison to be punished not entertained.

I truly believe that understanding and forgiveness would do so much good in some cases.

In my view, not all crimes are the same. They're committed under vastly different circumstances, with different intentions, pressures, and life stories behind them. To judge everyone the same way is dangerous. Yes, some crimes are horrific, and yes, there are people who are genuinely dangerous and must be closely monitored. But what about those who were backed into a corner? Those who felt they had no choice? What about those born into poverty and trauma?

Even in the worst of times, especially in the worst of times, that's when you've got to hold onto your faith and your hope with both hands. Without faith, without hope, life can become unbearable. They are the things that carried me through the darkest nights, the longest days, when grief or hardship felt like it might swallow me whole.

It was my faith, sometimes faltering, sometimes strong, that helped me survive when I had nothing. When I was broke, down to my last few quid, feeling lost. I always believed that there was still a way, that somehow things would work out. There was always a reason to keep going, even if it was just the smallest sliver of hope.

That belief, that stubborn insistence on hope, has shaped my life more than anything else.

My connection to the Church, especially to the Immaculate Heart of Mary Church on City Quay, has been lifelong. From my earliest days as an altar boy, through adulthood as a reader, I remained involved, tied to that place in ways deeper than tradition.

When I look back on those days, they seem simpler, softer somehow. Life felt less complicated. But maybe that's just nostalgia talking. Even so, I do think the sense of shared belief, of community, was stronger then. Today, it feels different. There's a stark contrast between the world we lived in then and the one we inhabit now. I don't think what's missing is just the Church, it's that sense of something greater, that sense of spirituality that connected us to each other.

Every day, I try to do my best to help others, to run a good business, to provide for my loved ones, to keep people employed, to offer a helping hand when I can. I know, deep in my bones, that I couldn't do any of it without my faith. I couldn't be the madman sometimes needed when facing challenges in my personal life. I couldn't be the court jester lifting spirits. I couldn't be the quiet support behind the scenes.

Without faith, I would have been lost long ago. God is my default. My safe place. And I speak to him often. Not always in formal prayers, but in the quiet conversations of the heart. There's a bigger picture, a divine plan unfolding for all of us, even if we can't always see it in the moment. And every day, I thank God, for another sunrise, another chance, another moment of laughter or grace. He's never failed me yet.

The truth is, Mattress Mick saved my life. And I don't say that lightly. After years, decades, of struggle, disappointment, and feeling like I was slipping further into the shadows, the birth of Mattress Mick was nothing short of a personal renaissance. It was like a spark in the darkness. Redemption, a wild, unexpected rebirth of hope and purpose at a time when I needed it most.

For so long, I had been drifting, caught in a cycle of failed ventures, broken dreams and mounting pressure. I had lost confidence in myself. I was tired. Worn down by the grind of life, and the sense that maybe, just maybe, my best days were behind me. But then he came along, this loud, lovable, outrageous character named Mattress Mick. A persona that began as a bit of silliness, a marketing stunt, a gimmick even, but ended up becoming something so much more than I could've ever imagined.

Mattress Mick wasn't just a brand. He was a lifeline. He gave me something to believe in again, something to fight for. He made people smile. And slowly but surely, I began to rediscover pieces of myself I thought I'd lost for good, my creativity, my sense of humour, my spark. Suddenly, I had a platform. A reason to get up in the morning with excitement instead of dread. He brought joy into my life, and into the lives of others too.

Looking back, I see Mattress Mick as a tribute, not just to my own rollercoaster life, but to my parents. To the people who raised me, who loved me, and who never gave up on me, even when I was at my lowest. I think about them often. I think about all the times I doubted myself, and how they always encouraged me to keep going. They had faith in me, even when I had none in myself. And now, I hope, wherever they are, that they're looking down and feeling proud of their son. Proud that I didn't quit. Proud that I didn't throw in the towel, no matter how tempting it was at times. I stayed standing. I kept pushing.

There's something to be said about being able to reinvent yourself, especially later in life when the world expects you to slow down. To fade into the background. Instead of fading, I came alive. I painted my name across Dublin in big, bold letters, sometimes literally, and I danced, shouted and sold mattresses with more enthusiasm than anyone thought possible.

I've done what I could. I'm still doing what I can. I built this life from nothing, from hardship, from failure, and I'm still standing. The original comeback kid. The world gave me lemons, and I made limoncello. Mattress Mick gave me a story worth telling. And I've loved every second of it.

Acknowledgements

Michael Flynn

Ladies and gentlemen,

I'm at a stage in my life now where I feel it's important to take a moment to sincerely acknowledge and thank the people who helped me get to where I am today. Because no journey is ever travelled alone, and mine certainly wasn't. I owe so much to so many, and today, I want to recognise them properly.

First and foremost, I want to thank my parents. They were exceptionally hard-working people who taught me the value of effort, resilience and family. My father was an incredible pillar of strength. Even now, all these years later, he is the 'chairman' of my company. His presence, guidance and spirit have stayed with me throughout my entire life, steering me through every high and low. Thank you, Dad. I hope you're proud.

Next, I want to mention my wonderful wife, Margaret. Margaret was with me every step of the way for over 40 years. She was the person behind the scenes, holding it all together, especially during the hard times and trust me, there were plenty of them. There were moments when we had next to nothing, when it felt like the walls might just fall in, but Margaret never wavered. She always told me to believe, to have faith and to keep pushing forward. Her support and belief in me were beyond priceless. I owe her more than words could ever fully express. I know Margaret is watching down on her girls and guiding them.

My daughters, Marina and Michelle, are my pride and joy. Throughout everything, they've been nothing but supportive. I love them to bits. They've been a huge source of strength and happiness in my life. Thank you both for being who you are.

I want to give a very special shout-out to my late sister Mary. Mary worked alongside me for an incredible 40 years. She stood by me through all the ups and downs, the tough days and the victories. I miss her deeply.

I also want to acknowledge my late brother, Brian. Although we weren't close growing up, he later became a massive help to me. I remember his support, and today, I thank him publicly for everything he did for me.

Also, I'd like to thank my sister, Catherine Flynn, who was a huge support throughout the years, especially when my wife passed. It will never be forgotten. Thank you from your big brother, Mick.

I'd like to express my eternal gratitude to Brian Doyle, the managing director of the Royal Trust Company, who gave me my first real opportunity. He took a chance on me when others didn't. I'll never forget that, and I'll always be grateful to him for opening that first important door.

When I started my business at the Northside Shopping Centre, I was lucky to have the loyalty and dedication of Alan Cusack and Paddy Kelly. They came on board early, stuck with me through thick and thin, and when we decided to build something new, the Mattress Mick brand, they were right there beside me, helping bring it to life. I genuinely couldn't have done it without them.

To the suppliers who supported me when I was operating the Northside Furniture Centre Limited, a massive thank you. Some suppliers turned their backs, but many didn't. And those who stuck with me through the rough times are now sharing in the success of the Mattress Mick brand. Loyalty is rare, and I'll never forget those who stood by me.

There have also been many friends along the way who stood by me when things got rough, who didn't turn their backs but instead lifted me up. I want to thank a few of them by name: Joe Landy, who I've known nearly all my life, Joe Byrne, Mal Deveney, Sean Cusack and Barry Murray. Each of them, in their own way, supported me when I needed it most, whether financially, emotionally or simply with a kind word at the right time. You don't forget things like that.

I'd also like to give a big thank you to Ger O'Connor and Paul Durgan who helped gather the photography for this book.

I must also thank my circle of friends, the lads I meet for a few pints, for a chat, a bit of craic, and most importantly, for their kindness. After Margaret passed away, they were the ones who kept me going. They offered me not just words but genuine warmth, and unwavering support.

I would also like to thank the Breakfast Club, made up of my great friends Gerry Byrne, Noel Plunkett and John Summers. We've met every Saturday for many years at Bram's Café in Marino for breakfast, and they have been my friends for over 20 years. Their friendship and support has meant a great deal to me.

Finally, a huge, heartfelt thank you to Josephine McCaffrey. Josephine wrote and directed the *Mattress Mick* musical. She poured her heart and soul into it and also wrote this, my autobiography. Without Josephine's talent, dedication and belief in my story, I wouldn't be writing this. Thank you, Josephine.

In closing, I want to say this: every success story has a cast of supporting characters. Mine has been blessed with some of the best people anyone could ask for. I hope I've made you all proud because you have certainly made me grateful beyond words.

Sleep well and thank you all from the bottom of my heart.

Cheers, Mick

Acknowledgements

Josephine McCaffrey

Working alongside Mick to tell his story has been a journey of late nights, emotional moments, exhaustion, laughter that turned into tears and tears that turned into laughter. I sometimes joke that I know more about Mick's life than he does, to which he agrees.

Through countless hours of conversations, interviews, memories and voice notes, I've pieced this book together with his full blessing and collaboration. My job wasn't to change Mick or polish him up; it was to capture him as he was and is.

I've sat with him through some of his highs and some of his heartbreaks. I've witnessed both the Mick the public sees, larger than life, the king of craic, and also the quieter, more reflective side of Mick, who has known real struggle, who thinks deeply, who prays often, and who holds his friends and family very dear.

What struck me most throughout this process wasn't just Mick's story, but the way he lives. I've seen him give money to the homeless. I've watched him stop mid-conversation to check on someone he's never met before. He gives out packets

243

of cigarettes to people sleeping rough, not because it looks good, but because he genuinely cares. That's the real Mick: always thinking of others, even when his own world has been upside down. And now, I'm lucky enough to call him my friend.

This book has been stitched together piece by piece, memory by memory, always with honesty and integrity. It's in Mick's voice, with his full approval, and with the invaluable help of his family, especially his sister, Catherine Flynn, and his daughters, Marina and Michelle. Their support, insights and openness have been vital. I'd also like to thank Mick's friends, Joe Byrne and Dean Scurry, who were gracious enough to share their time and help me understand Mick's journey better.

I'd also like to give a shout-out to a few others: my long-suffering mother, Margaret McCaffrey, who patiently read every draft, every paragraph, every sentence. She has read more books than anyone I know, and her wisdom and feedback were a constant throughout this process.

To my own friends and family, thank you for understanding while I disappeared for weeks at a time, buried in interviews and edits. I hope you enjoy reading Mick's journey from boy to man as much as I enjoyed bringing it to life.